the *Reset*

A HIGH ACHIEVER'S GUIDE TO FREEDOM AND FULFILLMENT

Your Step-by-Step Roadmap for Getting Unstuck

DR. TONI WARNER

THE RESET

A High Achievers Guide
to Freedom And Fulfillment

Your Step by Step Roadmap for Getting Unstuck

Dr. Toni Warner

THE RESET: A High Achiever's Guide to Freedom And Fulfillment
Your Step By Step Roadmap to Getting Unstuck

Contents originated from The RESET course, a coaching and educational experience provided by Bold and Balanced Coaching, a Toni Lynn PhD Enterprises Company
Toni Lynn Warner-McIntyre, PhD, MeD, MSW

Published by Brave Healer Productions.

Print ISBN: 978-1-954047-47-1
eBook ISBN: 978-1-954047-46-4

This book will teach you
why you feel trapped in your life and
how to get free.

WARNING: Once you begin, you can't unlearn what insight you gain from this process. For meaningful change to occur, disruption of old patterns has to happen. Before continuing, be sure you want to welcome a RESET and all that may come along with it into your life.

This book is dedicated:

To those who've inspired me and to those in pursuit of inspiration.

To the inspirers in my life, from close and afar, I thank you. I appreciate you. I and so many others have benefited from your teaching and your example.

To those in pursuit of inspiration. I believe in your worthiness, and I'm grateful for you. Inspiration is fueled from within, and I've set the intention for this book to help flame that fuel of internal desire so you can experience the feeling of being set free.

To my fellow achievers, doers, leaders, go-getters, working parents and caretakers who are out there pushing themselves to create a better world and a better self. I want you to know that ease and impact can be a part of your life experience. You're worthy of feeling free within your own lives. The immense amount of courage I see shine through those of you I get to speak to or work with, is humbling and inspiring.

Table of Contents

Introduction

Click. Click. Clickety, click. The sound of my fingertips rampantly tapping against the keyboard echoed throughout the whole first floor of my home.

I was sitting at my dining room table, staring at my computer screen. I'd been crunching numbers and building, then re-building my schedule so I could figure out a way to make it all work.

You see, just one year prior to this day, I'd opened up my own private practice as a psychotherapist. That same year, I'd also completed my PhD program. One year prior to that, I'd gotten our first family puppy and had my third baby.

Things were supposed to be stable now. No more schooling. No more late nights and long weekends of graduate classes while juggling full time work, motherhood, health issues and marriage. But, things didn't feel stable. Things didn't feel right. My mind, heart and soul were yearning for more.

Seemingly, the avenue to the more I'd yearned for had presented itself in an unexpected way earlier in the year. It was an avenue down a path that I'd never thought of going before. But, for some reason it felt so right. And so, I found myself sitting at my dining room table, trying to find a way to make time for this new thing, while maintaining my current workload and still be the present, involved mom I enjoy being. As I tapped and stared, then stared and tapped away at my computer, I was trying to find practical ways to justify doing this new thing that I knew would cost time and money upfront, without an immediate return. I was determined and secretly, I was scared.

I was scared my ambitious venture would stress my husband out and he'd get mad that there was yet another "big" (seemingly nonsensical) thing I wanted to do. I was scared I'd apply myself, invest my time and money, and then have nothing to show for it in the end. I was scared that if I started this thing, there was no going back. Failure couldn't be an option even though I couldn't guarantee what may or may not happen. *If I do it, I have to make it work.* I feared disappointment. I didn't want to disappoint myself. I didn't want to disappoint him. I didn't want to disappoint anyone.

On this particular day though, more than the fear, I felt the faith. Faith that this route was the one I was meant to go down, even if it meant taking risks, falling flat, being misunderstood or challenging myself in new ways. I felt the faith that the deeper impact and the larger income could both happen, with abundance, if I was willing to do this scary yet exciting thing.

Staring, vacillating my eyes back and forth from my screen to my notebook, I realized what I needed to do. I needed to take the leap. No, I wanted to take the leap. Despite the fear, my faith was stronger. I desired to leave my salaried position to open a second business so I could deepen my impact and income in my own ways, while still having time to be home with my children.

My heart pounded in my chest so loud that I'm pretty sure it could be heard from the second floor of our extended cape cod home. My palms were sweating. I couldn't bring myself to cohesively speak the words, so I texted them. "I can't build the businesses I want to build, make the impact I want to make, and be the mom I want to be, if I stay at my full time job. I have to leave. I want time to focus on building my businesses *and* be with the kids."

Was I asking for too much? Maybe I am a little nuts.

I hit send, and darn near felt like my head was going to explode. I'd sent the text to my husband. *I just finished my PhD, he's going to think I'm nuts. He'll never understand. He's gonna freak out and just want me to play it safe and stay where I'm at.*

Although the wait was brief, the pause was palpable.

What would he say?

I grew more anxious and then I heard the buzzing of the vibrations from my phone against the table. It was him. He responded. *Should I look?* I knew uncertainty and spontaneity were not his thing, which is why what happened next completely stunned me. He said: "Follow your heart"

What?! Seriously?!

Never had he ever muttered those words to me (or to anyone probably). I was shocked. I took a double look at the text to make sure I read it right. I have no idea what my face looked like at that moment but I imagine my jaw dropped. My butt felt like it was glued to the chair. I couldn't get up. I could feel my heart pushing against my chest. Immediately, my eyes welled up with tears and I cried. I cried tears of joy, of excitement, of love, of gratitude and of relief. Warmth filled my body from head to toe.

I had no idea where this new entrepreneurial road was going to take me (or us), but it was most certainly this moment on this day that solidified my decision to chart this uncharted course. This moment was one of the single most defining moments of my journey which would eventually lead me to creating the RESET and writing this very book for you.

Months later, I'd leave my full time work as a school social worker, emotional support counselor and consultant. I'd turn my attention to growing my existing private psychotherapy practice as well as pursue that unexpectant avenue through a second business—becoming a lifestyle success and leadership coach.

This was just one life-changing experience I had as a result of my own RESET. Where your RESET journey may take you is yet unknown. Regardless of what's going on in your life right now, you can expect the unexpected to happen if you take your RESET journey seriously.

And so I say welcome! Welcome to your RESET journey.

You're here, at least in part, because you want to feel better and clearer in some way. We all have decisions to make and habits to break; it's part of being human. We all tend to get stuck in habits, whether they're doing us any good or not. Certain lifestyle patterns and mental habits wind up preventing us from making and sticking with decisions that could lead to better experiences and outcomes in our lives, both personally and professionally. We stay stuck in old patterns most often due to lack of awareness or lack of clarity. Therefore, to help you get unstuck, this book will help you optimize both of these– your awareness and your clarity. Awareness about where you're actually stuck and why. Plus clarity about these two things as well as what next steps to take in what direction.

Choosing to open this book and apply it to yourself means that at least part of you is ready to explore and potentially commit to change. Maybe the change you want is big, maybe it's small, or perhaps you view it as somewhere in between. Regardless, there's something you want to improve or change in your life in some way.

The above is the case for most people at some point in life. While some decisions may feel easier to make, most people have a particular area that they tend to get stuck in time and time again. It has happened to me plenty of times.

Take this book for example. I've wanted to write my own book since I was a teen. I started at least a dozen drafts before following through on this one. Although I decided I wanted to write a book long ago, I hadn't decided exactly what I wanted to write about, or when I'd want to have it completed. I'd created a strong lifestyle habit of staying super busy with a ton of different things going on in my life at any given point in time. This busy-ness made it easy for me to not get committed to making the decisions I needed to make for my first solo book to get out into the world. It wasn't until I released a best-selling collaborative book in 2020, *The Wellness Universe Guide to Complete Self-Care, 25 Tools to Stress Relief,* that I finally committed to completing my own individual book in 2021. That book can be found at www.BoldAndBalancedCoaching.com.

Maybe you are not exactly sure what you want yet, but you definitely know that you want to feel more clear and fulfilled than you presently are. Or perhaps you just don't want to feel stuck anymore. Conversely, you may have already decided you do or don't want something, but you haven't yet fully committed to the steps needed to get there. Perhaps the details of those steps seem hazy or out of reach because you've got habits that keep getting in the way of moving toward the goal. Wherever you're at with all of that, you can bring it here and apply it to the RESET process.

I designed the RESET process to address my own experiences of vying for a reset because I wasn't feeling satisfied in my life; not personally and not professionally. I called upon my personal experiences, dove into the research, and pulled in my own professional experience as a psychotherapist and coach to distill the process into eight practical core concepts that are easily customizable and therefore widely applicable and beneficial to many. From this conglomeration, the RESET was born! As a result of these many years of effort, you get the benefit of saved time and turmoil as you don't have to figure out how to reset all on your own. However, please know that you get out of this process whatever you put into it. Should you choose to commit yourself to this process, I have no doubt you'll gain invaluable insight and great benefits along your RESET journey.

Using this book is one of a multitude of ways to engage in the RESET process. You can also go to BoldAndBalancedCoaching.com and view the current programs and services available for things like the digital self-paced or live coaching courses on the RESET as well.

Getting Started

I'm thrilled you're here! Wherever you've been, and wherever you're presently at in your life journey, it has brought you right here to this place with this book. Simply by choosing to begin here, you're one step closer to hitting your RESET button. That means, in a very meaningful way, you're already making progress.

While opening this book is one of the first steps, the real benefits come when you fully commit to the RESET process. If you're here, engaged, and willing to commit, then get ready for a unique journey. You've chosen to invest time and resources into learning how to hit your own RESET button, so you can get clearer on what you want and move in that direction with less stress as you enjoy more of life, work, and relationships! So, that is what we are going to do.

I tend to attract high achievers, optimal performers, impact-driven leaders, and out-of-the-box thinkers. If some variants of these titles resonate with you, you're in good company. I attract you because I, too, fall into the general characteristics associated with these categories (even though I'm not a fan of labels).

Maybe you've dabbled in self-development before, have done a lot of self-growth work or perhaps have chosen to more strictly focus upon development in the professional rather than personal realm. Regardless, you likely pride yourself on learning, growing, doing, and excelling.

If that's the case, you may relate to some or all of the following:

- You push yourself hard and like to get things done.
- You want to be able to do well at life, work, and relationships without feeling guilty, overwhelmed, or like you've lost yourself.
- You care about your impact; you have goals or big dreams.
- You often over-extend yourself, but it's exhausting so you want that to change.
- You've had experience with approaching (or crossing) your breaking point and have felt some combination of guilt, anger, anxiety or depression about it all, which is a cycle you don't want to repeat.

If you can relate to any (or all) of that, then you're in the right place.

As an achiever myself, I was addicted to action, avoided rejection, and firmly focused on goal achievement to prove my enough-ness. Ultimately, I outwardly accomplished a lot, but I burned myself out in the process. Even after getting myself out of burnout twice, I found I wasn't satisfied with the life I was building. I needed a reset but had no idea where to begin.

The inception of this book occurred during these challenging moments of my life before I ever even knew my story would go on to inspire transformation for others in such a powerful yet practically applicable way.

It's important you know this is not a *sit back or stand idly by* type of book or process. You'll minimally benefit from simply reading the pages. The impact comes from applying what you read and learn here. Apply it to yourself through reflection and incorporate it into your day-to-day life too. Although I recommend focusing on one core concept per week, an *ongoing* commitment to yourself is required to achieve the desired results.

If you want to maximize this RESET process for yourself, you can add the daily coaching lessons from the digital RESET course (www.BoldAndBalancedCoaching.com) or register for a live RESET coaching group if there's one currently open for enrollment. Both are great compliments to this book. Whether you choose one, none, or all of these opportunities is personal preference; it depends on how much accountability you want, need and are willing to accept, as well as how committed you are to the process.

Before you continue with this RESET process, it's important you make a personal commitment to yourself. Don't dabble. Some days will be easier to remind yourself to read the pages and engage with the prompts than others, but commit to yourself that you will stick with this process nonetheless.

To signify this commitment to yourself, you can sign the statement below. No one except you will know if you do it or not; this is a decision for you that only you can make.

I, _____ choose to fully show up for and commit to my own RESET process, for at least eight weeks. Even if I fall off track, I commit to picking back up again, because (below, indicate why this commitment matters to you)

_____

_____

_____   _____

My Signature   Today's Date

QUICK TIPS ON THE BEST WAY TO USE THIS BOOK

- Commit no less than eight weeks to this RESET process.

- Read one section and complete one prompt per day. There are enough to last you eight weeks.

- Do every exercise, prompt, and Point to Ponder.

- Write *in* this book as if it were the workbook for your life right now. Don't try to keep it "pretty." *Use* it, and it will benefit you greatly. **NOTE:** You may find this process so effective you want to repeat it for a deeper and deeper effect. In that case, buy a notebook exclusively for your RESET so you can keep coming back for more.

- Be honest with yourself at every stage. If you skimp in a section, go back and do it again.

- Reuse the RESET and apply it to any part of your life you want to focus on resetting but try to focus on one particular area at a time, each time you use the RESET process.

- Don't beat yourself up if you fall off track. Review what you did complete, and then continue along the journey from that point on.

Chapter One:

What Exactly Is the RESET Process?

I'd always felt like an anomaly. I'd wonder, *Why am I so different?* While part of me always knew there was a reason I didn't feel like I "fit in", there was another part of me that still felt hurt by it. It was like I felt both important and unimportant all at once. I wanted to find a place of acceptance in this world. I thought helping, doing or giving would help me feel that acceptance. You could often find me saying things like:

"Can I help you with anything?"

"I can do that."

"Nope, don't worry, I've got it!"

The voice in my head had convinced me that no one really cared what I had to say, they cared about what I could get done, how I could help, and what I could give to them. This is a large part of what attracted me to the helping and human service profession as a clinical social worker in the first place. I could help, give and do really well. I wanted to help, give and do for others. It made me feel useful. It made me feel valuable and needed. But this dishing out without receiving was off balance. And so, eventually, it made me feel exhausted, used, overworked, resentful and burned out.

In an effort to feel seen, accepted and successful, I learned how to use the attributes of over-achievement to find my way in this world. While working hard, sacrificing, people-pleasing, advocating for others and silencing my own needs to make way for what others wanted did all help me achieve a lot in life, I'd unknowingly become stuck in an unfulfilling cycle of over-doing.

This cycle followed me into adulthood and it wasn't just at work either, it was at home too. My relationships were mostly all lopsided and I'd made them to be that way.

"Fine, I'll just do it myself!" I'd mutter with intense irritation at my partner as I'd add yet another thing on while getting my daughter ready, making breakfast, paying the bills, pumping for the baby, cleaning the kitchen and getting myself situated for work in the morning.

I've got this. It'll get better. I'd tell myself. But the cycle of over-doing would continue.

Being the high achiever who got things done had gotten me to where I was, and so it made sense that it wasn't going to be easy to just suddenly stop being so busy all the time. The more accomplished I became, the more I wondered what was next. The next goal, the next responsibility, the next challenge to master, the next thing to prove. That is, until I realized how unfulfilling my life had become. It got to a point where no goal, no achievement, no amount of giving, doing or helping seemed to be enough. I wanted to feel more fulfilled. I wanted to feel free rather than trapped within my own life. I wanted to feel these ways, but I didn't want to lose my ambition. I didn't want to sacrifice my dreams. I wanted success *and* life satisfaction.

I distinctly remember one particular work experience that smacked me in the face and helped me realize that I was stuck in an overworked, over-achieving cycle that just wasn't serving me or my life anymore. I'd taken a 20k pay cut for a new job that was supposed to allow me a more balanced schedule after leaving a therapy position requiring me to be on call 24/7. I accepted the pay cut because quality time with my children was worth it to me. However, once I'd begun the job my ambition became evident. I was highly efficient and innovative. My supervisor, let's call her Janice, seemed to be a strange combination of both pleased and oddly suspicious of my performance. So, Janice called me in for a meeting and said:

"You'll need to stay after work hours to get supervision. Supervision hours are required for this position and no one can meet with you during work hours."

I reiterated, "Janice, I was transparent with you about the pay cut I'd be taking in order to say yes to this position. To help compensate financially, I provide consulting hours after work a few days per week before my kids daycare closes."

"You still have to do this." she said sternly. "This is your job and it needs to come first."

I was shocked. "It's not in the contract for me to work after hours. Supervision is included during work hours and if I meet after work hours it would cut into my ability to compensate financially for my family."

She was unwilling to budge.

I felt angry and anxious all at once. *What in the world? Is this really happening? Am I missing something?* At the time, it felt like I had no recourse. I just had to make it work, like I always did.

My relationship with this supervisor would grow to become so anxiety-provoking that I'd start to experience panic attacks on my drive into work and I'd question my own judgment. I made the decision to leave after completing my first contract with that place of employment, and I promised myself that I would never allow my professional life to negatively impact my home life or health like that again.

It took years before I truly understood and fully followed through on that promise to myself, but I now am at a place in my life where I can be my ambitious self without having to over-work, people-please or unnecessarily sacrifice. I am able to live in this more balanced, free and fulfilled way, because I learned how to RESET my life without losing myself, my dreams or my drive.

The RESET process I share with you in this book, is one that was birthed from real, raw, true experiences within my own life, as well as those I've supported (none of whom are exclusively represented in this book, for confidentiality purposes). I was as stubborn as I was giving, and so no one could have told me that I could get unstuck by doing X, Y or Z. Truth be told, no one could have told me I was "stuck." I was in denial about that for a long time. Chronic busy-ness has a way of making someone believe they're not stuck because, well, they're always in motion. But, I was stuck, and I needed to experience the possibility of living unstuck myself; only then would I buy into it as a viable option. This is one main reason why the RESET is designed to be an experiential process for you. I don't want you to just take my word for any of this; I want you to experience your RESET for yourself.

This process is broken down into eight core components (interchangeably referred to as concepts) intended to help you break through barriers that have been keeping you stuck, so you can experience more overall life satisfaction. In this book, these eight core concepts are spread across eight consecutive chapters. One core concept will be discussed in each chapter, although you'll find overlapping principles applied throughout. Each core component builds on the others, so it's best to read the chapters and execute the exercises in order. I recommend spending a minimum of one week focusing on one core concept at a time. This translates to doing one chapter per week, for a minimum of eight weeks.

My goal for each chapter is to break down the core concept in a practical and digestible way, often using examples from my own life journey. Other times, I share a synopsis of stories from work I've done as a professional. For anonymity's sake, no client stories are exact to any particular person; rather, they're a combination of true experiences crafted to illustrate a relevant point or concept.

Stories are powerful, and I've learned there is great benefit to sharing my personal challenges and triumphs with others who are ready and willing to listen and learn. Some stories may resonate with you more than others as you seek to understand the core components and apply them to your life. That's great! Conversely, your experiences may be vastly different than what's presented here, and that's absolutely okay too! What's most important is you take the time to read, reflect, and apply what's presented in this book in a personalized manner so you can gain the maximum benefits your RESET journey has to offer you at this time.

EXPERIENCE TEACHES MUCH BETTER THAN WORDS.

The RESET is set-up to serve as an experiential learning process.

There's so much information available to us nowadays; it can easily result in information overload. My desire isn't to introduce you to more of that. We don't necessarily need more information. What we need is transformation, and transformation only happens when we've integrated new or different experiences into our brain, body, soul and lifestyle. I designed this RESET book to extend beyond mere cognitive understanding of certain perspectives or concepts because I don't want you to focus on just collecting more information. I want you to truly *integrate* the learnings from this book in a meaningful, life-enhancing way. For this reason, the processes in this book will ask you to go deeper than you've likely ever gone before.

The most powerful teaching opportunity I can present to you is the opportunity to experience these concepts in your own day-to-day life. The exercises (which I call Points to Ponder) are therefore a vital part of your RESET process. To create a powerful, customized experience, it's essential you engage with each of them. Come to the table with an open mind as you read, reflect, and respond to each section, and it will pay off. Don't skip any Points to Ponder or other personal reflection and application sections, as you'll only be doing yourself a disservice.

Furthermore, research demonstrates the brain loves repetition; it would do you no good to try to rush through this book without pausing for review or reflection. Review and reflection are missing from so much of our daily lives. Trying to "get it all done" at once is a cramming method popularized in our culture but is counterintuitive and doesn't support deep, meaningful change or growth. Repetition might feel annoying to you at times (I know it has for me), but it's a requirement when it comes to self-growth and sustainable life enhancement. Every day, allow yourself ample time to experience and reinforce each concept and take time to reflect intentionally.

Research also demonstrates that focusing on too much at once reduces performance, motivation, clarity, efficacy, and more. This is another reason why I recommend you focus on only one Point to Ponder per day and no more than one chapter per week. It's okay if it takes longer, but it's not going to serve you well to go faster. Allow the tasks, guidance, and prompts to marinate throughout the days and week to maximize the benefits.

As I mentioned earlier, each component is necessary and builds upon the one before it. It won't be helpful to look ahead at other chapters. Focus on the section you're in. If you fall off track and choose to pick back up later, it may be best to start again from the beginning. Commit to yourself that you'll show up for your RESET process every day, preferably for the next eight weeks or more. It won't require a lot of time each day, but it will require the decision to regularly and deliberately show up. That's how you get results.

Dedicating ten to thirty minutes each day to read and reflect is a good ballpark time block to commit to. Each exercise is different and each one includes an affirmative statement for you to repeat to yourself throughout the day to help reinforce that weeks concept. Some people may choose to take more time with certain exercises, and that's okay.

Since everyone is at a different place in their lives, supplemental materials are mentioned within a few chapters. These are intended to deepen the RESET process for those who may need or desire it. Any offerings mentioned are supplemental and not required to gain benefits from the RESET process. You can find these materials on my website at www.BoldAndBalancedCoaching.com. Feel free to take them or leave them. You'll notice powerful results either way.

CHAPTER RECAP

You'll see chapter recaps at the end of each chapter. These brief sections will provide you a quick synopsis of some of the important points from each chapter. These are helpful to reference throughout your RESET journey.

CHAPTER INSIGHTS

Each chapter has a chapter insights section which provides space to go deeper into journey-enhancing reflections. I encourage you to take full advantage of these sections. Add onto them with additional reflections that may come up for you as you complete each chapter.

RECITE AND AFFIRM

At the close of each Point to Ponder is an affirmative statement for you to read and recite for yourself, in order to further reinforce the concept you're working with.

Core Concept One: Getting Motivated

*"Motivation: the reason or reasons one has
for acting or behaving in a particular way."*

— Oxford Online Dictionary

I've always been a driven person. I set my mind to something, and I get it done.

By thirty, I'd achieved my major goals in life. I'd had my third baby, completed my PhD, two master's degrees, was an experienced clinician, owned my own car and home, had gotten married, and had a full-time salaried position (with good insurance) doing what I went to school for.

I should have been satisfied.

I was no longer a young, single mom living off loans and rationing diapers like I did when I was twenty-two. I was no longer stuck in the toxic work environments where I'd physically, mentally, and emotionally deteriorated in years prior. I wasn't constantly fatigued like I had so often been for many years in my life.

It wasn't easy to get through those hard times. I'd worked hard and achieved what I had worked hard for. Yet, even after all the accomplishments, there was still a void.

I'd been to burn out twice before, but I could feel I wasn't in burn out anymore. I wasn't in it, but I was very aware that I didn't want to go back to it. I didn't even want to flirt with that idea. I could still feel the memories of it viscerally, if I allowed myself to mentally go there. The anger, the heart-ache, the resentment. No, I was glad I wasn't living in that space anymore and I sure as hell wasn't planning on going back to it. So, if I wasn't in burn out anymore, why didn't I feel more satisfied with my life?

I didn't feel like I was just surviving, but I didn't feel like I was thriving either. I was still hustling in life, but not nearly to the extent nor with the level of intensity as I'd been accustomed to before. I guess I was . . . existing.

I was living but not feeling like I was blossoming. It kind of felt like I was moving and standing still all at once.

I knew my work was meaningful. For the most part, the people I worked with valued my expertise and my support. I worked in the schools, which was the schedule I'd always wanted while parenting my young children. I loved being a mom; and while there were some people at work who weren't fans of mine, I had more than a handful of amazing colleagues and I was really good at my job.

Still, there was something off. Something more was calling for me. I was kind of content but not really fulfilled.

I often wondered to myself:

Is there more? What more is there?

I've gotten everything I've worked for, why am I not satisfied? What's going on?

How could I want more after working so hard to get to where I'm at?

Do I even know what I really want anymore?

While I never labeled myself as a conformist, I certainly did (and I do) try to do well. I'd always try to put my best foot forward because I wanted to be successful but I also didn't want people to be upset with me. So, I'd done all the things I was "supposed to do" to be considered a "good successful adult." I got the degrees, paid my own bills, did the extra-curriculars, volunteered, helped as much as I could and worked multiple jobs.

I proved countless nay-sayers wrong.

I *achieved* the goals.

I *looked* successful.

I had come a long way.

I'd put in time and worked hard.

But there was still this deep sense there was more for me. Much more.

Don't get me wrong; things were not all sweet, smooth, and shiny in my life. My marriage wasn't where I wanted it to be. There were some people at work who seemed to have so much negativity, low energy, lack of empathy, or judgment towards me, and I had to figure out how to navigate it all.

Still, people live like this or worse all the time. Right? I'd mentally remind myself after a full day of work, kid events, making dinner, prepping for psychotherapy clients and not seeing eye-to-eye with my partner.

I mean, how many people do you know who just stay where they're at because it's familiar or because they'd worked hard to get there? There are plenty of people who don't like what they do, who they're with, how they are, etc., but they just "deal with it" because "that's life." There are plenty of people you've probably met (maybe you're one of them) who're burned out, but they stay and keep doing more of the same anyway.

So many people just stay where they're at, living like they're living and doing what they're doing because:

They think they *should*. Or.

They think it's too late to change it. Or.

They're too scared to try something new. Or.

They're supposed to be happy with what they've got. Or.

They're concerned it's "too risky" to leave. Or.

They invested so much to get there it seems like a waste, bad, wrong, or dumb to go in a different direction. Or.

[Insert potential fear here…]

You can probably relate to some aspects of this experience. Most people can.

Have you ever felt like you've: done all the things, or worked really hard to get where you are, or checked off all the boxes, or defied all the odds, only to get to a place where there was still something that seemed off, or not enough?

To me, living this way was like settling in life and I didn't want to settle.

How in the world can we feel motivated to try or to do something different if we are stuck in the muck of the familiar and too scared to take the risk required for change to happen?

At the point in my life I've described above, I'd already spent years learning to manage anxiety and depression. I'd gone in and out of burnout a few times and truly accomplished many things.

I thought I had taken chances.

I thought I had done something "different" than most.

So, why did I feel so unfulfilled?

It just didn't seem to make sense.

Perhaps you're at a place in your life where you feel "off", behind, stuck, stagnant, constantly stressed or overtaken by your schedule and life's demands. Maybe you suspect something needs to change, but you're not sure what. Maybe some variation of all of this is what brought you here to the RESET.

Good!

I know that sounds like a weird thing to say, but I mean it. Good!

Why?

Because that means something bigger, better, and more for you *is* in store. Just as I learned there was for me.

Although I had no idea where to start, I did know I needed some momentum. I needed some motivation to just start somewhere, somehow. That's why the first core concept of your RESET focuses on how to begin getting motivated. Although the process I take you through may seem contradictory at first, I assure you clarity will eventually follow.

As ironic as it may seem, getting motivated to rev up my change process required me to get more clear on what I was no longer okay with in my life. Since I wasn't clear on what exactly I *did* want, identifying what I *did not* want would at least give me a foothold on where to start. To do this, I had to take a deeper look at the stuff that felt "off" for me —the stuff I wanted to be different. It didn't feel great at first of course, but it did ultimately help lead me to feeling more motivated for charting a different path forward.

I started revving up momentum by identifying the things that were draining me, things I didn't like, or things that otherwise made me feel bad. Some of those were:

- I didn't like dealing with certain coworkers that constantly talked behind other people's backs and judged my colleagues or me for being different from them.
- Although I had worked on it before, people-pleasing was still showing up more than I'd like, which was anxiety-provoking.
- I didn't like feeling I had to work more to make more, especially after finally getting myself out of burnout.
- I was annoyed by the political red-tape my colleagues, administrators, and I had to deal with at work, which often didn't align with my values or weren't in the best interest of those we were trying to help.
- I was frustrated by the gap in communication among the various tiers of staff and leadership at work, especially knowing well-intentioned people were suffering as a result.
- I didn't like feeling unfulfilled and disconnected in my marriage.
- I didn't like worrying about work stuff bleeding into my family time.

Common statements I've heard from others (which signify it's time for a RESET) are:

"I just feel like there has to be more than this."

"I'm sick and tired of being sick and tired."

"I just want to feel happy."

"I want to feel like I'm making a difference."

"I'm tired of feeling like I'm on that hamster wheel (or in the rat race) of life."

"If I keep going like this I'm going to burn myself out."

"I'm just not satisfied."

"I'm done burning myself out."

"I work so hard only to feel unappreciated."

"I feel like I'm going in circles. What's the point?"

Maybe a variation of one of these phrases fits where you are, or maybe you're just tired of feeling overwhelmed and being constantly stressed. Perhaps you're exhausted from being in constant "on" or "go mode" all the time. Or maybe you're feeling pulled in too many directions because your schedule is always full, and there's never enough time. Whatever it is for you, it's time to stop ignoring it.

Ignoring it won't help; it'll make it worse.

It's time to stop trying to avoid those thoughts. Stop pushing them away. Stop the blaming or justification for staying where you are or expecting someone or something else to swoop in and change it for you. For as long as you do that, you will not RESET. You'll stay on this course, and it will continue to repeat various undesirable versions of itself in different ways throughout your life.

Two common questions underlying all the above statements are: *Is better even possible for me and my life?* or *Shouldn't I just be happy with what I've got?* And the answer to the first one is absolutely, unequivocally yes! Better *is* possible. The answer to the second one is both yes and no. While it's important to find appreciation with where you're at, you have to allow yourself to dream and want more if you're to actually experience more in your life. Both are true.

Even though examining these thoughts isn't easy (in fact it can get pretty freakin' uncomfortable, to say the least) it helps build the motivation needed for a RESET to happen. I knew I wanted to experience something different than where I was at, even if it meant taking a few risks. I wanted to live a life that felt more deeply meaningful to me, even if it felt hard or meant everyone else may not understand. Some people call this a course correction; I call it a RESET. And I had to choose to commit to a RESET for myself in order to see things change.

Yes, there was some tough love in the above there for you; and yes, it was needed. Now it's your turn to decide. What will you commit to?

POINT TO PONDER #1
Exploring the Yuck

Reflect on what brought you here and desiring a RESET at this time in your life. What has been going on that you don't like or want to change? What is it you no longer want or desire to be different?

Here are some prompts you can ask yourself: "What do I want to see change?" "What is draining me?" "What am I sick and tired of?" "What is it I don't want?"

Using the space below, write down whatever comes up. Try to be as specific as possible.

Throughout your day today, if you notice something you no longer want, don't try to change it right away; simply jot it down. Jumping into action before gaining motivation and clarity about what next steps to take can often keep you stuck in the same loop. For now, we explore by observing and taking note.

Recite and affirm the following statement, at least three times today (starting now). Plug a reminder into your phone so you don't forget: "When I notice what I don't want, I become more motivated and clearer on what I do want!"

CATALYST TO CHANGE.

A catalyst can be defined as a thing or event which stimulates change or action to occur. And all too often, we humans don't change until a jarring catalyst comes by and urges us to do so. A looming divorce. A health scare. A financial crisis. That's because our familiar is our zone of comfort, and regardless of how unfulfilling or dysfunctional it may be, the familiarity of it makes it feel less scary than the uncertainty that lay outside of it. This is why many people say change didn't happen until "I hit rock bottom", "I couldn't bear it anymore", "I gave up" or "I had no other choice". Sometimes, it even gets to the extreme where it's a matter of life or death.

An effective way to get started with a RESET and not stay stuck, is to gain enough motivational leverage that change feels significantly more appealing and meaningful than your familiar (aka keeping things the same). For this, you need a catalyst.

Without a meaningful catalyst, we humans tend to just kind of "stay put" or "deal with it." Staying put isn't necessarily wrong or bad. It's often just more appealing than putting in the work to do something else, especially if the something else isn't clearly known or can't be guaranteed to work out well.

However, "staying put" or "just dealing with it" for too long keeps us stuck; it reduces our motivation to progress in a truly meaningful way. A catalyst often grabs our attention enough to make "different" seem more appealing than continuing to "stay put" or "just deal with it."

For example, I could have easily stayed put in my salaried position with a school-based schedule. I was really good at my job, and I did generally like it. I had a group of people I'd gotten along with well. It was a good job. I was helping people. It was stable.

I could have told myself to just deal with it.

I could have ignored the "off-ness" creeping in and tried to avoid the growing lack of fulfillment feeling I'd been having.

But, if I'd done that, I'd eventually need one of two things:

1. stronger and stronger distractions to help me numb or avoid the growing "off" feeling (any attempt to do so would only serve as a band aid, like seeking ways to get a higher salary, working to add other credentials to my name, etc) or,

2. a bigger catalyst to happen in my life (likely showing itself through an impact on my health or relationships, like what happened when I was in burnout before) to further prompt me towards some kind of change.

I know it may seem strange to actually go looking for a catalyst, but you likely won't have to look that far. There's a reason you were attracted to this book, and that reason may be a strong enough catalyst for you to build up and use here. Besides, if you don't build a case for a catalyst yourself, life has a way of creating a catalyst for you. It certainly did for me.

Since I burned out before, I knew ignoring how I felt would only make me feel worse. Eventually, something would have to change. I'd already experienced my body suffering from exhaustion and neglect in those former burn out years. I wasn't going to go back to constantly thinking:

Why am I always so fatigued?

There must be something wrong with me.

It's got to be a medical condition; it doesn't make sense that I feel this crappy all the time.

Since I'd formerly let things get a lot worse before addressing them in my life, I decided I wouldn't wait until things got so extreme again. So this particular time around, the unfulfilled feeling was enough of a catalyst to get me considering something different. I didn't know what "different" would be quite yet, but I knew I didn't want to go back into burnout. Two of my catalysts were a) I didn't want to keep living feeling unfulfilled (especially after working so hard to get to where I was), and b) I didn't want me or my family to have to deal with me going back into burnout again.

Whether or not you choose to stay put or move out of certain situations, like a relationship or a workplace, is *not* what you have to decide right now. Action before reflection can lead to more frustration. Instead, get curious about why you came to this book. Is that reason strong enough to keep you committed to change? Is there a catalyst that rivals any tendencies to "stay put" or "just deal with it"? If you can build the case for a meaningful catalyst now, it won't need to keep getting bigger and badder to get your attention later. Often, the best way to do this is to recognize how the things you don't want are making you feel.

POINT TO PONDER #2
Building A Catalyst Case

Over time, I realized it wasn't just particular situations I didn't like about my life; it was how I was *feeling* about those situations that caused me the most frustration. Among other things, I didn't like feeling unfulfilled, stressed, or misunderstood. It's the same when I work with clients. While they may want certain circumstances to change (like their impact, income or relationship situations) when they come to me, the main pain is typically *I don't want to feel bad anymore*, or *I just want to feel better*, or *happier* or *more fulfilled* (which is just another way of saying I don't want to feel the way I feel; I want to feel differently).

Without awareness of a strong enough catalyst, we can convince ourselves to keep going as we have been and wind up tolerating a whole lot of yuck (yes, that's the technical term). As a result, the yuck keeps coming. We keep numbing, distracting, tolerating, justifying, or avoiding it. Still, it keeps coming, and we keep letting it pile up, even though we don't like it.

To get your initial motivation revved up even more, you often have to get fed up with where you're at and how it makes you feel. If you ignore how you feel, it's hard to build a case for the meaningful catalyst that may help propel you forward here. You know something is meaningful to you based upon how you *feel* about it. Building the case for a catalyst can help build up your motivation for change and get you ready to commit to your process of getting unstuck.

Look at the list of things you don't want from the first Point to Ponder and write down how they make you feel. Then reflect on how those feelings might be impacting you and certain areas of your life. What might the costs of sticking with this familiar be?

DON'T WANT	HOW I FEEL	IMPACT/COST
Ex. To get burned out again or to spend most of my adult life doing things I don't find joy or fulfillment in doing; I don't want to settle	*Ex. Unfulfilled, scared I'll make the wrong choice, guilty that I've worked so hard to get here and still feel like there's more, or different for me out there*	*Ex. I'll probably get resentful or burn out again and then I'll get more irritable. That hurts me, my kids and my husband. It'll probably effect my work relationships too.*

Recite and affirm at least three times today (starting now). Plug a reminder into your phone so you don't forget: "When I notice what I don't want, I get more motivated and clearer on what I do want!"

FOCUS EFFECTS FEELING.

As I started to buckle down with noticing what I no longer liked or wanted in my life, I realized how much my point of focus was affecting how I felt. What I tended to focus on was impacting how I felt more than I had previously cared to admit.

Here's a seemingly silly example, but it's one that happened in my life:

I'm a smiley person. I like to smile. When I'm out and about, I'm typically smiling. I'm not talking about smiling at inappropriate times, like when someone else is hurting. Just, in general, smiling feels good to me, so I naturally gravitate toward doing it. However, there was a period of time before my initial RESET when I'd get frustrated because I'd smile at someone, and they wouldn't smile back at me. I'd take it personally and think something like, *Wow, that was rude. I at least deserve a smile back. It's not that hard.* Then I'd wind up feeling annoyed for smiling, which was completely counterproductive since smiling was supposed to be something that felt good.

At the time, I hadn't realized how much my focus was impacting how I felt. In my internal dialogues, I'd blamed my frustration on the other person. If they had smiled, I could feel good. But since they didn't, I couldn't feel good. I had become so focused on what I did not like and what I wasn't getting in return, that it actually made me feel bad about smiling. I'd start to second guess myself when I smiled.

As simple as this example may seem, when I switched from focusing on what I didn't like about other people's behaviors, or what I wanted but wasn't getting, I started to feel differently.

I had to change my focus; focusing on other people not smiling back was just making me feel worse. That point of focus didn't fit for me anymore. I didn't want smiling to become associated with negative social experiences, and I definitely didn't want to feel bad about myself for a simple smile.

I knew I wanted to feel good about being the smiley person I was (and am). I wanted to smile when I felt like it and help focus on the benefits smiling had for me and potentially for others. I didn't want how I felt about myself to be so easily and negatively impacted by how others acted. I needed to let go of focusing on their lack of smiling to make space for me to feel good about it. So, I shifted my focus to my own reasons for smiling, and the benefits smiling can bring to people who are open to it.

By intentionally letting go of other people needing to respond the way I wanted, I made space for me to do what came naturally to me and also feel good about it! As a result, I felt happier and less bogged down when someone didn't smile back at me. I was never smiling to get a specific response from someone anyway. I smiled because I like to smile; it's one way to spread joy to others. Ultimately, I realized I could choose not to focus on certain things outside of my control–like when other people didn't act the way I wanted them to.

How about you? Are you willing to let go of a certain focus to make space for something that feels better to you?

POINT TO PONDER #3
Where is My Focus?

Where you place your focus in any given situation affects how you feel about it. Since we can't control other people's actions (or lack thereof), it often works against us to hyper vigilantly focus on the behaviors we don't like. The same is also true regarding situational outcomes. We can't control all outcomes, and when we focus on how much is out of our control, we then start to *feel* out of control! Giving these things all or most of our attention is draining and frustrating, at the very least!

Take time to reflect on certain things outside your control that you've been or are currently focusing on, which ultimately make you feel worse. Even the small things matter here, as small and as simple as someone not smiling back at you.

Now, when you focus on the thing or behavior that makes you feel bad but is outside of your control, ask yourself: "How have I been dealing with this?"

Based on your response to the above question, further contemplate:

Is there a particular behavior, thought process, or attitude I have been engaging in (like getting frustrated with a stranger, snarky with a partner, or road raging at other drivers) that no longer fits for me? Am I satisfied with how I've been reacting? Am I willing to try swapping it out for something a bit different that may fit better for me?

Write down what comes up for you. Continue on with this line of inquiry and ask yourself "What thoughts, feelings, or experiences are coming up the strongest for me right now?"

_____

_____

_____

_____

_____

_____

_____

_____

_____

_____

_____

_____

_____

_____

_____

_____

Recite and affirm at least three times today (starting now). Plug a reminder into your phone so you don't forget: "When I notice what I don't want, I'm motivated and clearer on what I do want!"

PAYING ATTENTION TO FOCUS AND BOUNDARIES.

It took time, but I continued to notice what I no longer wanted. I continued to get curious about what I was focusing on, how it made me feel, and what focusing patterns no longer fit for me. You, too, have been practicing these things as well throughout this chapter.

As I put more effort into practicing these pieces, I noticed some annoyance. I discovered I'd still sometimes find myself getting frustrated when other people didn't act the way I thought they should. If I had to put so much effort and intention into resetting myself, it seemed only fair for them to do the same.

Right?

I mean, why won't they just up-level too? Can't they see I'm trying to make some changes here?

Maybe as you move through this phase of your RESET, you have some variations of thoughts like:

I'm trying to be positive, why aren't they?

I'm putting in so much effort, can't they just try even a little bit harder?"

This person (situation or thing) is making it impossible for me to . . .

I've had some similar thoughts before too. But these kinds of thoughts were sucking up my time and mental energy. So again, I had to decide if it was a focus that was working for me to continue with or if it was a focus I needed to re-evaluate and shift in some way.

While it's normal and human to have these kinds of reactions at times, it's never helpful to maintain focus on frustrating, blameful, or resentful types of thoughts indefinitely. It's emotionally and mentally depleting. I certainly was not about to keep giving up my mental energy all willy-nilly like that. I was trying to get intentional about my life, and I didn't want this annoyance of observing other people's behaviors and attitudes to consistently stand in my way.

It was one thing to shift my own thoughts, attitudes, or behaviors when they no longer fit for me, but what about when other people's stuff was coming up? If I couldn't control other people, but I was more aware of how I felt about their behavior, what could I do? I had come to a point where I had to figure out what I was going to do to help myself reduce this pattern of focusing on other people and letting it affect how I felt in such a strong way. If I didn't, I knew my RESET was likely to significantly slow down, or even come to a halt.

I recall experiences with a particular colleague during a time when I wanted to RESET. This person seemed to be bothered by me; not all the time, but often enough. Progressively, as work stress amped up, so too did their apparent annoyance of me.

"Why are you so nice? It makes me wonder if you have some ulterior motive or something?"

I hesitated on how to respond. *Really, my nice-ness is being called into question?*

They'd gossip around me and assume I'd be judging them because I didn't contribute to the workplace gossip scene.

"I feel like I can't gossip around you because you never gossip; it's like you're just sitting there judging us."

I wasn't sure why my colleague would think that, since I never said anything about their gossiping up to that point. Their comment felt like a personal jab. *Was I making a face or something?* I wasn't sure if I'd given some kind of non-verbal indication of judgement, so I checked in on my facial expression. Nope, no rude face or anything. Still, my assurance that I wasn't judging their character based solely on the gossip didn't seem to change much of anything. They'd wind up holding these assumptions against me and then used them as ammunition to gossip about me to others in the workplace.

And indeed, my colleague was right about one thing; I didn't like gossip. I had been on the receiving end of gossip at various points in my life in times past, and it never felt good. I never found it productive or helpful, only harmful. Therefore, to the best of my abilities, I chose not to gossip.

However, I wasn't judging this individual as a whole person simply based upon their gossiping. It was clear the culture we worked in had its own gossip cliques; thus, that one individual was of no significant exception. Nonetheless, I'd seen other wonderful sides of my colleague. I saw they cared about the impact of their work and when less stressed, really had some creative ideas to contribute. Plus, I was in the midst of a RESET which was further incentive for me to get more deliberate about what aspects of them I'd chose to focus upon.

You see, we may not be able to control other people (and thank goodness for that because I would *not* like other people to control me). But what we can do is shift what we choose to focus on about them (or the situation), because where we focus affects how we feel. Of course, this is easier said than done, and sometimes it doesn't seem possible to focus on a different aspect of someone or something. At times, the negative stuff has just been going on for far too long or has become way too extreme, and so it's just too hard to shift focus. When this is the case, we might try shifting our focus to someone or something else that's more pleasant in general. But sometimes, not even that seems possible or practical. Sometimes, the person or the situation is just so in-your-face that any attempt to shift your point of focus can feel like a violation of sorts.

For example, remember the colleague I just mentioned? Well, the gossip and assumptions grew. After making statements negatively geared towards me one too many times, I decided I'd no longer tolerate it. It felt like a violation of my boundaries to allow the increasingly inappropriate accusations to continue without saying anything about it. At that point, the accumulation of what was being said was not only untrue, but how it was being said was construed to defame my character, and it didn't seem like it was stopping any time soon. I decided it was something I needed to address head-on.

"Hey, would you be available for a phone call later? I wanted to talk with you about some stuff that seems to be going on with us."

They agreed, and we later got on the phone.

"I want you to know that I appreciate the work you do. But if I'm honest, it seems like you've been really upset with me lately. I'm not sure why. But, the comments about me not gossiping and judging you all for it, the accusations about my nice-ness being some kind of ulterior motive – those were hurtful. I don't think you meant it to be but…"

I started to get teary-eyed at this point, and was grateful I was on the phone so no one could see my face.

"Growing up I was on the receiving end of gossip a lot, and it didn't feel good. It was really painful for me, and so I really pride myself on not gossiping about other people. I've not seen it go anywhere good, so I don't do it. At the same time, I'm not sitting around gossiping about you or anything like that. I'm not trying to make you feel uncomfortable, but I'm just not comfortable gossiping, so I don't say anything when others do it around me. There's no ulterior motive on my end."

The other person seemed less guarded by this point in the conversation, "I get it. You know we just work in such a toxic place that it's hard to know who to trust…" They went on to apologize and their tone shifted from defensive to receptive.

Shifting your point of focus off of who and what you can't control doesn't mean you can't have boundaries. In this instance, a boundary of mine was being crossed. I needed to say goodbye to keeping my mouth shut. Holding back on using my voice and setting boundaries to "keep the peace" in this way, had unintentionally turned into a pattern of self betrayal. As Dr. Martin Luther King Jr so vehemently expressed, there "comes a time when silence is betrayal". While Dr. King was speaking to macro-level matters, his message rings true at the individual level as well.

Although I felt some fear, I still chose to pick up my cell and discuss the situation with my colleague. I tried my best to be honest rather than accusatory, explaining how I felt and why. I addressed the concerns I had and communicated a boundary around the untrue statements and assumptions that had been tossed around about me.

"I get that things are really rough with certain groups and people here right now, but I'm not going to engage in gossip, not about you or anyone else. I'd appreciate it if you didn't include my name in any gossip as well. I don't think it's going to help much of anything anyway. We're supposed to be working together and I'd like us both to be able to do that more comfortably."

The conversation continued on, and we were able to amicably end the call. It wasn't easy, and I could not guarantee this other person would respect the boundary I set. What I could do was honor and communicate my own boundaries and re-assert them if and when the issue were to arise again.

Sometimes, the efforts we make to reach out and communicate a boundary are not heard or understood by the other person. When defenses run too high, it makes it hard for any communication to effectively get across. That can feel really frustrating. At the same time, it can feel empowering to know you have choices in these kinds of challenging situations. While you can't force anyone to behave the way you want them to, you can practice shifting your focus so you can feel better, bit by bit. You might try telling yourself something like, *I can tell they aren't receptive right now. I can always talk to them later; but right now I'm going to choose to just step away.* You can practice different ways to set a clear boundary and consistently hold yourself to honoring it. You can also adjust boundaries in need of adjusting.

In the particular circumstance I shared above, the other person did seem to hear me and did apologize. My boundary came with vulnerability, and helped my colleague more easily relate to me. By directly communicating how I felt, what I expected and why, my colleague seemed to feel more connected with me, not less. I can assure you this conversation did not stop that individual from ever gossiping again, but it did radically shift how we interacted with one another.

Sometimes, saying nothing and reorienting focus is the best option available in dealing with the undesired behaviors of someone else.

Other times, the answer is to speak up and put a boundary down more clearly and consistently than previously communicated.

Sometimes, the way to deal with it is to create distance from the situation, thing, person, or group.

There is no one cookie-cutter way to shift focus or deal with boundary-setting. Even if you aren't struggling with particular relationships right now, you can apply these ideas to any area of your life where you want a RESET.

For example: Say you want to change your relationship with food, but you're frustrated that you've put in the effort and nothing has changed. You can't immediately change the number on the scale. However, you can set a healthy boundary for yourself while still shifting what you focus on about the food you eat. For instance, instead of setting such strict dietary boundaries that even the thought of eating a piece of cake results in you mentally bashing yourself, you might instead adjust your dietary boundaries to set yourself up for success. Setting a clear boundary for yourself, while adjusting it as necessary, will allow you mental space to shift your focus when there's an opportunity to eat a piece of cake. As a result, instead of criticizing yourself about eating the cake, you may instead reinforce the boundary to yourself with more compassion, saying something to yourself like: *This is delicious! I can eat this and still choose healthier options at other times. I've chosen to eat the cake for this special event, so I'm going to fully enjoy every bit of it!* This different approach to setting boundaries with yourself would be more sustainable and therefore more effective in the long-run. This kind of boundary-setting is one that you internally set with yourself, and it is a matter of intentionally shifting your focus.

When you're focused on things that bother you and that you can't directly or imminently control, boundaries become an important part of the equation. Say your frustration is aimed more at your body than your food choice, you may shift your focus from judging your physical appearance to appreciating what your body has and does do for you. When looking in the mirror, instead of criticizing yourself you may set a boundary for how you're allowed to speak to your reflection. Rather than mentally bashing yourself, perhaps you say one true statement of gratitude about your body anytime you look in the mirror. Something like: *Those legs get me around to where I need to go every day. I'm sure grateful I have this part of my body to support me each day.*

I know it might sound silly to talk to yourself in this way, but you're talking to yourself anyway. We all are. We have thousands of thoughts per day and most of them are just repetitive ones that we keep recycling because we're so used to using them. Boundary-setting provides guidance for others to know what we are and are not okay with, yes. But, it also provides guidance for our own minds. Getting better at setting clear, consistent yet reasonable adjustable boundaries, helps us to better establish communication as well as to better steer the focal point of any given conversation or situation within ourselves as well as with others.

Applying this method of shifting focus and setting boundaries in such a way can feel too cliché or too abstract for some. However, when you apply it specifically and give it a try with consistency, it makes a big difference— whether you're doing this with a person, a situation, or otherwise.

When you've been putting in the effort and aren't seeing all the results you want when you want, there is no one right blanket answer on what the exact best thing to do is going to be. However, it's certain that shifting your focus in some way and setting clear and consistent boundaries will always be necessary parts of the process.

POINT TO PONDER #4
Assess and Set Boundaries

Boundary assessing and setting is hard for many people. Being so used to focusing on certain people, situations or things in a certain way and then challenging that way of focusing is equally difficult. So, this exercise is a challenging one that will take time and practice to understand and integrate in a meaningful way.

Do some self-exploration.

What boundaries am I missing or are not effectively being communicated to people in my life? Am I focusing too much on not liking other people's behaviors? Is there behavior happening that I'm no longer willing to tolerate? What boundaries might help with this?

Take a few minutes to write down what has come up for you here.

What have I been focusing on that makes me feel bad, and could use a different boundary strategy? What do I need to say goodbye to or put a boundary around—either with myself or someone else?

_____

_____

_____

_____

_____

_____

_____

_____

_____

_____

_____

_____

_____

_____

_____

_____

_____

_____

Although we need to put down boundaries with others, sometimes the person neglecting our boundaries the most is our very own self. No matter what, you're the one who, first and foremost, needs to get clear on what you'll no longer tolerate. This is *not* about controlling anyone else in any way, shape, or form. This is about getting clear with yourself first, about what boundaries you may be neglecting or not clearly communicating. Once you're clearer on that, you can start incorporating it into your life more. A lack of boundaries will lead you to experience less of what you ultimately want, while clear and consistent boundaries will help you experience more of it!

Write down your thoughts about and reflections to this below.

BONUS CHALLENGE.

As you move through your day today, rather than jumping to do something about these areas right away, be a bit of a detective. Come back and take note of what you observed; reflect on these notes to get even clearer about where you first want to make a shift with your boundaries.

_____

_____

_____

_____

_____

_____

_____

_____

_____

Recite and affirm at least three times today (starting now). Plug a reminder into your phone so you don't forget: "When I notice what I don't want, I'm motivated and clearer on what I do want!"

CHOICES.

Okay, at this point, you're much clearer on what you don't want. But now what?

As much as I realized I needed to get more specific about what I didn't want in my life anymore, it wasn't a super easy or comfortable awareness process. You're probably noticing this, too, as you engage with each Point to Ponder.

The more focused I became on what I didn't want, the more I thought about how bothersome they were. If I focused on how bothersome they were too much, I felt worse. The worse I felt, the more easily irritated and bogged down I could get by the day-to-day parts of life. Since we now know focus impacts feelings, this effect makes sense.

But the ripple effect of how we feel doesn't stop there. How we feel goes on to impact how we behave, and I was no exception to this rule. Our behavior is directly impacted by how we feel. When we feel stressed, agitated, or some other challenging emotion, we tend to have certain default ways of dealing with it all. Our default ways of dealing with stressors and challenges are often much more reactive than we'd like them to be.

When I felt overwhelmed, I'd often have less patience for myself and sometimes for other people too. I'd get frustrated when I felt like I was putting in a whole lot of effort to make things better, but not really see the same effort being put in for me by others in return. Sometimes, if I were upset or angry, I'd withdraw and not want to be around anyone.

At other times, it kind of felt like I was in victim mode. It was feeling like things were happening *to* me or *against* me, and therefore, they all felt out of my control. This victim-like feeling led me to hunker down and go into "super-independent-woman" mode, depending only on me, myself, and I. But I didn't want to feel like I had to go it alone in life forevermore. Feeling misunderstood and alone was part of why I wanted a RESET in the first place; so, I knew I didn't want to continue with that old pattern of reacting to certain thoughts and feelings I was having.

We all have default ways of reacting. However, you're here, continuing your RESET journey because you, too, know you want a change. You want to up-level some part of yourself or your life. You know you don't want to stay stuck in unhelpful or unhealthy patterns in your life anymore.

That matters. It really does.

And it will require some introspection on your default ways of reacting when your emotions aren't feeling good.

No matter how uncomfortable it got, I knew I didn't want to keep slipping back into the isolating armor I was used to putting on throughout my life. If I was to really RESET, I had to notice the discomfort. I had to confront the challenging feelings I felt as I focused on what I didn't like and no longer wanted to tolerate.

So, I did, and then I found myself at a crossroads. I could continue focusing on what I didn't want and do nothing about my old ways of reacting to it. Or I could notice how looking at what I didn't want made me feel, get clear on how I was reacting to it all, and then choose to do something different about it. Noticing the reaction is one choice, but doing something about it is another choice. These are two intertwined yet distinctly made choices.

In your own unique way, you'll find yourself at a crossroads at some point too. You'll be faced with the decision to choose the same or a different way of reacting.

If you're engaging in your RESET by reflecting on the Points to Ponder and implementing the reflective points throughout your day, you'll start to become more aware of your emotional reactions to things, situations, or people you're displeased with. As you do, it's important to notice the agitation, irritation, pain, or frustration arising as you observe what you don't like. When you do notice how you tend to react, you get a chance and a choice.

You get a chance to more deeply explore and therefore understand the specifics of what you're reacting to and why. But more importantly, you get a chance to better understand how you deal with challenging emotions that need to be dealt with and whether it's working for you.

With this information, you will get to make a more informed choice. Which choice you choose to move forward with will be up to you! Here are the umbrella categories for the most common choices available to us all:

CHOICE A: AVOID OR DISTRACT

You can try to numb or ignore the challenging emotions; many people make this choice. You may turn to drinking, eating, overly-caretaking for another, overworking to stay "busy," or some other form of avoidance, to help *not* pay attention to it all. Just as you start to notice how you feel, you try to avoid the crappy feelings with myriad forms of distraction. This option creates a pseudo-sense of control, so it becomes easily addictive. These momentary distractions create long-term, unhealthy habits, which ultimately lead to more issues. But it's an option.

I had chosen this option many times in the past. Be it through jam-packing my schedule to stay "busy," binging and purging, cutting, creating a new lofty goal or "to-do" to avert my focus to. I used these avoidance methods to the extreme at various points in my life, and they created unhealthy coping patterns for me that showed up in so many different areas of my life.

Sometimes, distraction *is* an appropriate and effective choice. In moderation, healthy forms of distraction can provide a needed respite so you can come back and tend to it when you're in a less reactive state of mind. However, if you find yourself distracting so much that you never return to tend to your own emotions or needs, then this choice will eventually backfire.

CHOICE B: DO NOTHING AND FOCUS NEGATIVELY

Another option is to focus on what you don't like, assume it'll always be that way, and just let the negativity dictate your direction. That often looks like allowing a challenging emotion, like anger, disgust, or shame, to become your universal point of focus. Over-use of this choice may lead you to often feel like people or things are working against you, or at the very least, they are never working for you. Choice B often does not feel like an option. Instead, it feels like the *"hand I was dealt."* It feels like it just happens, it's unfair, and there's nothing you can do about it. This will leave you feeling powerless.

Abundant use of Choice A or Choice B will leave you feeling stuck. If you're having a strong reaction to reading either one of the above options, there is likely something about them that's resonating with your way of dealing with life. Many people unknowingly choose one of these because they don't want to or don't know how to deal with the challenging emotions that are bound to arise if they were to try something different. If this is the case for you, that's okay. Now that you're bringing more awareness to the habit, you have a better idea of what's going on within you. This will help you to more actively and more intentionally choose differently as you continue along your RESET journey.

CHOICE C: ACKNOWLEDGE AND SHIFT

The third option is to notice the agitation, irritation, pain, or frustration that comes up. Acknowledge what it feels like and why. Then, use it! Use it as a catalyst and as a filter to get clearer on what you want.

There is a reason why feelings come up when you focus on what you don't like. It's because there is something there that you care about. There's something in the mix of what you're experiencing that actually matters to you or is in some way connected to something of emotional significance for you. If you really didn't care about any of it, it wouldn't be worth the trouble it's been causing in your life. The real emotional significance isn't always immediately obvious, but it's there; it does exist.

Raising awareness about how we feel when things hurt or seem out of control is hard and scary because it often brings the unknown with it. The unknown is where most of us are bound to feel some level of vulnerability and lack of control. The obvious response to avoid going to the "unknown" (aka "out of our comfort zone") is to retreat into what's familiar, even when it's not what's healthiest or most desired.

Most of us don't realize vulnerability is required for real change to happen. Vulnerability does not feel ideal and sometimes doesn't feel safe. So, we distract or avert to something that feels like a viable distraction, is familiar, makes us feel in control or generally feels safer in the moment.

However, as Brené Brown says: "Vulnerability is not winning or losing; it's having the courage to show up and be seen when we have no control over the outcome. Vulnerability is not weakness; it's our greatest measure of courage." It takes that kind of courage to be vulnerable and feel those crappy feelings if we really want a RESET.

Although this awareness process is likely to feel uncomfortable, it's a part of the process that can't be skipped. This awareness process made me more conscious of how

I'd been dealing with my emotions. I was avoiding them by staying busy. When I slowed down to acknowledge how I was feeling, of course, it didn't feel great. But it gave me the information I needed to shift how I'd been doing and seeing things for so long.

Now, I could choose differently. The awareness that came from that acknowledgment helped me realize I had other choices, even when I'd previously thought I hadn't. Having other choices made me feel less stuck and more hopeful. If choicelessness leaves us feeling trapped, having choice is like removing the binding chains. It feels freeing!

Choice C invites challenge and vulnerability, yes, but it also invites profound change and growth.

It's vital you get familiar with what you have been choosing and what you want to choose moving forward.

POINT TO PONDER #5
Challenging My Choices

I invite you to get vulnerable with yourself today. Go back to Point to Ponder #2 and review the strong feelings that arise when you focus on the things that you don't want, don't like, or no longer want to tolerate in your life. Below, add any additional feelings you notice as well.

_____

_____

_____

_____

_____

_____

_____

_____

_____

Next, explore how you've been dealing with these feelings. Ask yourself:

"What patterns do I notice about how I do or don't manage hard things and challenging feelings?" "Which option do I tend to use the most? The least?: Choice A—Avoid or Distract, Choice B—Do Nothing and Focus Negatively, or Choice C—Acknowledge and Shift?"

_____

_____

_____

_____

_____

Get curious and ask yourself:

"How is this working for me?" "Am I open to trying a different way? Why or why not?"

_____

_____

_____

_____

_____

_____

_____

_____

_____

_____

_____

_____

_____

_____

_____

_____

_____

Recite and affirm at least three times today (starting now). Plug a reminder into your phone so you don't forget: "When I notice what I don't want, I'm motivated and clearer on what I do want!"

It's freeing to have choices!

CHAPTER RECAP

Getting motivated is about helping you commit to a change process that makes a difference. This requires noticing the things you don't like about what's going on in your current reality. It also requires a willingness to explore possible reasons why the commitment matters more than continuing with the old stuff. That's why you spent some time building a case for a catalyst in this chapter.

Noticing what you don't want can be both powerful and painful. I wish I could tell you change could happen without discomfort, challenges, or pain, but I would be lying to you. A RESET is a call for changing, upgrading, or enhancing some part of your life. That will require some discomfort, challenge, and, for many, some painful times too. It's all part of the process. Don't worry; the *whole* process isn't intended to be that way. For most, however, this exploration is necessary to create the leverage needed to initially get motivated enough to step outside of the familiar.

CHAPTER INSIGHTS

Committing to your RESET is a primary part of the life enhancement puzzle. Starting to look at some of the reasons why you want change can help you get motivated. As you look at things you don't like, you'll start to notice what you focus on is impacting how you feel, which in turn affects your choices. This means how you feel matters. In upcoming chapters, you will continue to build from these foundational ideas.

Take a moment to reflect and write out any insights that pop out to you from this chapter. Here are some questions you can ask yourself to begin:

"What felt hard for me to think about?" "What felt annoying?" "What did I strongly want to avoid?" "What did I feel most strong about?" "Was there anything that felt confusing for me?"

Despite the challenges, ask yourself: "Do I choose to renew my commitment to this RESET for myself?" Be clear about why you choose what you choose here.

_____

_____

_____

_____

_____

_____

_____

_____

_____

_____

_____

_____

_____

_____

_____

_____

_____

Recite and affirm at least three times today (starting now). Plug a reminder into your phone so you don't forget: When I notice what I don't want, I'm motivated and clearer on what I do want!

Chapter Three:

Core Concept Two:
Enhance Motivation With Clarity

When I looked up the definition of clarity, a few strong words popped out: "cleanness" and "transparent". Vocabulary.com described clarity as "Clean water running down a mountain..." It went on to read "If you bring clarity to a situation, you help people see what really happened by clearing up misunderstandings or giving explanations." In this chapter, we seek to enhance motivation by gaining greater clarity. In the process of gaining clarity, we often find ourselves revisiting the past. As any past experience is revisited by you, know that it's not for the sake of "digging up old stuff". This deeper awareness and clarity process affords the opportunity to help bring about a different way of seeing and understanding what was once hard to see or understand.

Still, you may be wondering, *So what if I know what I don't want? How does that help me?*

Well, it's very helpful and can bring greater clarity for you. For one, by the end of this chapter you won't be focusing so much on what you don't want anymore! Instead, you'll use your increased awareness of what isn't wanted to gain clarity and step into what *is* wanted. You can do this by flipping over your "don't wants" and getting curious about what is on the other side of them—your "do wants!"

With my newly found clarity, I no longer felt like I needed to hold onto everyone else's stress or try to fix everything for everyone else, especially at the expense of my own health and happiness. I knew I didn't want to feel irritated with my partner as frequently as I did. I also knew I didn't want to keep myself so busy that I wasn't feeling fully present with my kids when we were together. I didn't want to feel as lonely as I had felt for most of my life. I didn't want to work myself so hard, only to feel unfulfilled.

Knowing what I didn't want was an essential place to begin; it helped me sort and sift through the stuff of my life in a curious rather than complaining way. If you've allowed yourself to engage with the processes so far, you'll now be able to more clearly and effectively excavate what you actually *do* want more of.

What you "don't want" served as a jumping-off point. The distinctions identified in your exploration help you to say, *Hey, this thing in my life doesn't feel good or right to me.* From there, you can begin to lean toward the other end of the spectrum and explore what *does* feel good and right to you.

Core concept two, which is delineated in this chapter, is an incredibly important step in your journey. While core concept one helps to get motivation stirred up, staying indefinitely focused on what you don't want will lead you to feel worse, more out of control, and will eventually fizzle up your motivational juices. Core concept two will help you use this initial motivation to clarify what does feel good so you can begin to experience more of that instead.

I had to get up close and personal with myself to ask honest questions and give honest answers throughout my entire RESET process. You'll be tasked with doing the same. In this chapter, you'll be going deeper and deeper into the process of flipping your "don't wants" to identify your "do wants," and noticing how it makes you feel. This process will help you enhance your motivation with further clarity about why this RESET matters to you and your life.

CLARIFYING WHAT YOU WANT.

Clarity and motivation are the leverage you initially need to hook into to stick with your RESET process. That's why we want to bolster your clarity and motivation even more by going deeper into what you want and how you believe it'll make you feel to experience it.

Using your "don't wants" and how you don't want to feel as a starting point, you'll start to further dissect what you do want and how you do want to feel.

Some things I realized I didn't want throughout my RESET were:

- To work in a toxic work environment
- Passive-aggressive, one-sided, or codependent relationships
- Work stress and commitments getting in the way of quality time with my kids
- Feeling like I have to do everything exceptionally and by myself
- To feel like crap in my own body every day
- Restless nights

- Money stress (and it adding stress to my marriage)
- Chronic exhaustion

All of those things felt bad and were things I did not want to experience regularly. Focusing on all of those at once made me feel worse. I knew I needed the awareness from the previous process, but I also knew I had to shift from where I was to move forward. I didn't want to feel stuck again.

I shifted to using what I didn't want as a filter for what I did want, and surprisingly, I started to feel less frustrated, clearer and more in control! To do this, I had to flip my "don't wants" into "do wants." This is a process that may take time and repetition, depending on where you're at in your journey. However, if you do it with honesty while allowing yourself to really notice the feelings coming up during the process, the payoff is beyond worth it!

I will share some examples with you:

A "don't want" that I felt frustrated and stressed about when I focused on it was, *I don't like dealing with coworkers that constantly talk behind other people's backs and judge me or my colleagues for being different from them.*

So, I flipped this exact dislike around as if to look at the opposite end of it. I came up with something like, *I do want to focus on surrounding myself with people who are more honest and positive.*

Another area I felt strongly about was, *Even though I've addressed it before, I'm still worrying too much about pleasing people or what they think of me. It's draining me, and I don't want to be drained by people-pleasing anymore.*

When I flipped this "don't want" on its head, I came up with: *I do want to be able to be myself around people, regardless of their judgment of me.*

Here are several other examples, which are not uncommon:

- I didn't like feeling like I had to work more to make more.
- Flipped to- I did want to make a meaningful impact with my work *and* live abundantly.
- I was annoyed by the political red-tape that my colleagues, administrators, and I had to deal with, which often did not align with my values or the best interest of those we were trying to help.
- Flipped to- I did want to focus on how I could help professionally, in an ethical way.
- I was frustrated by the gap in communication among the various tiers of staff and leadership.

- Flipped to- I did want to use my skills to help close the gap among leadership tiers.
- I didn't like arguing with my partner.
- Flipped to- I did want better communication in my marriage.
- I didn't like worrying about my work stuff bleeding into my family time.
- Flipped to- I did want to have consistent boundaries with work and fun time for family.

As you read some of these examples, notice what comes to mind for you. If you feel strongly about not wanting something in your life, then you must care about how that circumstance, relationship, or experience is impacting you, directly or indirectly, in some way. If you didn't care, it would not bother you so much.

As an example of what I mean, consider the laundry or dirty dishes in your home. Perhaps you live with someone who doesn't seem phased at all by the laundry buildup or the dirty dishes piling up in the sink. Meanwhile, it really bothers you that the dirty dishes or dirty laundry is building up. You may be the person who doesn't like the laundry or dishes building up. So, you don't want that to keep happening. It bothers you because there is something about the situation that holds meaning for you. The pile up doesn't hold the same meaning for the other person, so they aren't bothered by it. Same situation, but two different people, two different perspectives, and therefore two different experiences about the same circumstance. I use this example partly in gest; but this is actually a very real issue for plenty of people. This example offers a way to easily conceptualize how different people can feel different ways about the same thing because different things hold different significance for various individuals. You feel different about things because of the meaning they hold for you.

Let's flip some "don't wants" to "do wants" in this example situation:

"Don't want"—to be the only person who notices the dirty dishes and dirty laundry building up and then have to clean it all up by myself all the time.

Flipped to a "Do Want"—to receive help with the dirty dishes and dirty laundry more regularly and frequently to avoid the piles.

A "do want" can't be written as a negative. Writing a "do want" as a negative is still focusing on what you don't want. A "do want" must be written as an affirmative statement. If it feels tricky for you, it's okay. This just means you're more used to focusing on what you don't want in this particular area of your life. As you practice focusing and filtering differently, over time, you will notice a difference in the outcome both mentally and emotionally.

An example of a "do want" written in the negative is: I do want my partner not to be so messy and unaware. This is not going to be a beneficial way of focusing on what you want. Don't write your "do wants" in the negative. A struggle here may mean you'll want to write these out in the negative at first and then move things around until you can find a more affirmative way to state what you do want.

POINT TO PONDER #6

Flip What I Don't Want to Find What I Do.

I Don't Want...	*Flipped to I Do Want...*

Recite and affirm at least three times today (starting now). Plug a reminder into your phone so you don't forget: "I love exploring what I really want; I'm worthy of happiness and health."

Did you take the time to engage with your last Point to Ponder? It's an important one that can't be skipped or glazed over. For some, this exercise will feel amazing. For others, it may feel confusing, and yet for others, it may feel frustrating. Whichever way you feel is acceptable. It's all part of your process. The key is to continue to follow this RESET process consistently with an open mind, an open heart, and a willingness to learn and experiment.

DAYDREAMING DIFFERENTLY.

One of the most fascinating things about our minds is how powerfully they can work both for us and seemingly against us. Now, our minds never actually want to work against us, but it can certainly feel that way sometimes, can't it? In this section, we're going to tap into one often misunderstood way your mind can powerfully work for you, to support your RESET process—with your imagination.

I know, I know. Not everyone will hop right onboard the imagination bandwagon-I certainly didn't at first. You may feel curious or excited about the idea of bringing your imagination into your RESET. Conversely, you may be thinking *"What!? Imagination? I want real-life change not some make-believe figment of my imagination that only exists in my head!"*

Yes, of course we all want to see the tangible outcome play out in a super concrete, easy to measure type of way. I get it. I did too, but the truth is we can't force that. It's all a process. When things aren't going all that well in certain areas of your life, there's a lot to be said for leaning into your imagination to get an idea of what feels good to you. To paint a simplistic example, consider any modern-day thing you use now, but which didn't exist 10, 20, 50 years or even 50 decades ago. You could probably come up with a long list of things that exist now, but didn't exist in the fairly recent past, couldn't you? Cell phones, high-speed internet, micro-chips, smart televisions, etc. All of these things started out as ideas. They originated from someone else's imagination. Now of course the examples I listed are related to the invention of physical objects, but the power of imagination stems beyond this. If we are willing to imagine it, our imagination can actually help us create new experiences in our lives. Although I initially scoffed at the idea of using my imagination too, I found it really is powerful, and science backs that up.

Neuroscience and other related research have demonstrated that when we use our minds to imagine in a way that elevates our emotions, the emotional parts of our brain don't know whether the experience is happening in real-time or not. The emotion-oriented parts of our brain just focus on feeling the experience. These "feeling" parts are different then the parts that focus on the sequence of time or logic. As a result, the more you connect a visualization (imagination) in your mind while genuinely feeling an elevated emotion, the more your mind becomes accustomed to that experience.

We can easily see this play out when we feel anxiety about something that hasn't happened yet. We create a scene in our mind of something bad, wrong or scary that we don't want to happen, and we feel bad about it *now* even though it's not happening right now. You can use your imagination to condition your mind using any elevated emotion – be it positive feeling, or negative. In this section, we are going to use the power of your imagination to strengthen your RESET by pairing it with elevated emotions that feel positive to you.

This may seem a bit abstract or "far-out" for some who are used to using their analytical mind a ton. That's okay. It was for me too. I encourage you to release some skepticism and give it a try. Know the goal isn't to dissociate or try to live in a dream state forever; that's not going to be healthy or effective in the long run. Instead, the general aim here is to begin to feel and therefore start to believe that more possibilities exist for you. The more you imagine what you want in your mind, while associating (real, not fake) feel-good emotion with it, the more you'll come to believe other possibilities could be true for you.

Have patience with yourself as you entertain the idea of marrying your imagination with what you want to see change in your life. It takes time to get used to using your imagination in this way. After that, it'll take time to move your imagined concept or experience into your day to day life.

After some initial resistance, I did begin visualizing what I wanted more and more vividly. For me, it kind of felt like daydreaming, but on purpose. Although the intention was for it to feel good to daydream about what I wanted, it didn't start out that way easily or immediately. I didn't automatically jump into daydreaming about what I wanted and then magically feel better. In the beginning, I'd try to visualize what I wanted to experience, like a smooth day with my husband and a fun time together as a family. I would *not* feel the benefits of visualizing the experience because my attention shifted right back to how much it wasn't happening right then and there. It felt like there was way too big of a crevasse between my daydream and my current reality. I reached too far, too fast.

It took some time to realize daydreaming was most beneficial when it didn't feel so far away or impractical to me. I needed to start dreaming from a bit of a more practical place and gradually scale up to the big stuff. If you feel any resistance to using your imagination like this, find a way to start small before building your imagined daydream up more.

One way I started smaller was by noticing how little parts of what I loved about my daydream were already happening in some subtle way. Like when my partner would help with something he hadn't usually helped with before, I'd try to notice that more. When I'd notice these small moments, it helped me connect with my daydream more. It didn't feel so far off. I could then incorporate those kinds of subtleties into my daydreaming. This made my daydream feel much more possible.

Sometimes it felt too hard to daydream on a specific topic. If I hit that point, I might try to switch to a topic that was generally easier for me to feel good about. This way, I at least gave my mind and emotions a healthy and enjoyable respite from focusing on stressful or undesirable aspects of my life for a brief period. Over time, I started to feel good when I'd visualize more of what I wanted to experience. I also started to notice little intricacies of connections between my daydreaming about what I wanted and my day-to-day life. This excited me!

The kind of visualizing we're talking about here can be a helpful way to connect with what you want and how you want to feel, even when things aren't exactly there yet. Of course, we can't live in a daydream (nor are we trying to). But this kind of visualization practice uses the power of our imagination, plus our desires, to help us get clearer on what we want to experience more of in our lives. As a result, we mentally and emotionally become more aligned with what we want, and the impact of that plays out in tangible ways too. Plus, we get to feel better moment to moment along the way!

Getting curious about what it would be like to experience more of what you want helps you feel it and believe in its possibility more. The more you engage with the possibility of not just daydreaming about your RESET but believing it can happen for you, the closer you move towards it.

POINT TO PONDER #7
Imagination Station

Get up close and personal with *you*. Ask all questions of yourself honestly and commit to answering them honestly, too. Today, allow yourself to daydream about what you do want. To help with imagining this, ask yourself questions like: "What might it look like?" "How might I feel?" "What might I observe differently in my day-to-day interactions?"

Write down any thoughts or feelings that come up as you allow yourself to imagine more about this. Don't force it here; just get curious with yourself. The ability to tap into your imagination and begin to paint a clearer picture of what you actually do want, is a strong indicator as to whether or not your RESET will unfold for you.

As an additional prompt, you may ask yourself *what would it be like if . . .*

Recite and affirm at least three times today (starting now). Plug a reminder into your phone so you don't forget: "I love exploring what I really want; I'm worthy of happiness and health."

What was it like for you to imagine or daydream about what you do want? How did it feel for you? Was it easy or hard? The experience will be different for everyone, but regardless, you'll need to revisit the exercise more than once to reap its benefits fully. You can jot down additional reflections here:

Daydreaming about what I really wanted was hard for me in the beginning. I had a very strong side of me that was skeptical because it was very oriented towards the more practical, tangible and measurable things of life. This skeptical side of me was hesitant about trusting that my imagination could help my life in any significant way. My skepticism was one of the reasons why when I'd initially imagined what I wanted, I'd almost immediately get mentally interrupted by thoughts of what had realistically just been getting in the way of it all. Or, I would imagine how I wanted to feel, and then I'd envision something going wrong or it not being able to last long. Thankfully, I chose to try and keep an open mind and open heart about it, so my ambivalence was temporary.

If any hesitation, confusion or frustration was the case for you too, that's okay. It's not an uncommon starting place. Play around with your imagination to find what feels good for you. Resistance to daydreaming your desires will decrease in duration, intensity, and frequency over time if you continue to incorporate this piece of your RESET process with a willingness to learn and try new things.

Through this imagining process, I gained more clarity about what I liked and how I wanted to feel. This clarity helped me feel more motivated to make some changes over time. I was not just mired down by the stressors of my life. Instead, I was connected with my desires; ones that mattered to me personally and which felt good. These dreams and desires opened up new ideas and possibilities for me. I was lit up and connected to my desires in a way that felt good. This helped me move from a place of motivation to inspiration, which is a much more powerful space to be in.

REWIRING YOUR BRAIN USING THE POWER OF EMOTIONS.

Once you've made the initial commitment to begin, the hardest part of trying something new or different is to stick with the process. As you move toward greater clarity and increased motivation about your RESET, the most challenging part will be to trust that sticking with the process will bring your desired results—even when things aren't going exactly as you anticipated they "should."

Believe it or not, connecting with your feelings in the way I outline within this book helps you reduce the frustration and stress of sticking with the process. That's because connecting with your feelings in this intentional way helps you to rewire your brain.

You've already begun the journey of rewiring some thought processes in your brain by bringing an awareness of what you do *not* want into your consciousness without trying to fight against it. You've been practicing that by engaging in the exercises within this book. You'll continue to use your increased awareness as a jumping-off point to clarify and connect with your deeper desires. As you do so, you'll more powerfully rewire your brain by connecting with your feelings differently than you have before so your brain can support you in a healthier and more effective way.

Are you ready to dive even deeper?

Yes?

Let's do it!

Whether you think of a RESET as a course correction, a goal, a desire, or like starting a new chapter, you want to experience a RESET for a reason that matters to you.

Don't you?

Some people want to lose weight because they think they, or someone else, will like them more at a different size. Some people want to get married or find a partner because they believe they'll finally feel wanted and happy once they have one. Others may want to better manage their schedule so their partner will stop nagging them so much. While yet others may want to hit a certain salary or get a certain promotion because they believe it'll make them feel better about themselves or prove to someone else they're successful.

I've found it increasingly interesting how we humans seem to too often think *if this thing changed,* then *everything would be better* or *fixed* in some way. I was certainly no exception to this belief. I set goals because I believed once I achieved them, things would be better, and I'd feel better.

It makes sense why most of us achievers believe this. Our system is set up that way. Think about it. Most of our lives go something like:

I can't wait until I get to high school; it'll be so much better than middle school. Life will be so much less stressful.

I can't wait to finish these exams; then, things will be so much easier. Life will be so much less stressful.

I can't wait until I graduate; then, I can finally do what I want. Life will be so much less stressful.

I can't wait until I get my degree; then, I can finally get the kind of job I want. Life will be so much less stressful.

I can't wait until I get this salary increase; then, I can finally afford to buy the house (or car or wedding) I want. Life will be so much less stressful.

I can't wait for this vacation; then, I'll finally have some time off. Life will be so much less stressful.

I can't wait until . . . then . . . life will be so much less stressful. Then I'll be happy and feel better!

The loop is unending!

Although there's nothing inherently wrong with goal setting, there is an issue with believing you can only have more time, less stress, and feel better about yourself once your goal is achieved. The issue happens when goal-attainment becomes the primary path to living happy and healthy. The happier and healthier life doesn't feel feasible because new goals keep on being set. The goals or *I can't wait until*...kind of feeling, just keeps on going. The loop plays on repeat, and you keep chasing the desire to feel better but never really feel better for more than what seems like fleeting moments.

I was so guilty of this!

This loop is often what leads to resentment and burnout.

Unfortunately, this common cycle does not break down on its own. You either have to deliberately change it, or something dramatic or traumatic in life has to happen to serve as a catalyst to the change. No one wants to wait for something dramatic or traumatic to happen, so how do you break the cycle deliberately? You start by connecting the dots between what you don't want, what you do want, and how you desire to feel.

Remember the example I gave about the dirty dishes and the dirty laundry in the beginning of this chapter? The one person wanted to receive help with the dirty dishes and dirty laundry more regularly and frequently. The affirmative statement about what that person wants to happen identifies the outcome, or what they circumstantially want, but it doesn't go deeper as to the emotional implications and impact that lay beneath. If we take into consideration that the person feels frustrated and unappreciated when thinking about the dirty dishes and laundry, we can use this information to identify more of how the individual *does* want to feel. Again, we can flip the don't wants to help narrow down the do wants. Instead of feeling frustrated and unappreciated, this person may want to feel more supported and appreciated at home. See how I focused on the feeling and not all the nitty gritty details of the situation here?

Notice what this example brings up for you. Here are some more examples to help stimulate thought around this:

- I don't want to work in a toxic work environment.
  - I DO want to *feel* more fulfilled by the work I do each day.
- I don't want to experience passive-aggressive, one-sided, or codependent relationships regularly.
  - I DO want to *feel* more supported by my relationships.
- I don't want work stress and commitments getting in the way of quality time with my kids.
  - I DO want to *feel* more present with my kids.

- I don't want to have to do everything exceptionally and by myself.
  - I DO want to *feel* like I have room to breathe and relax.
- I don't want to think I look like crap in my own body every day.
  - I DO want to *feel* proud of my body and feel good about how I take care of it.
- I don't want to have restless sleep every night.
  - I DO want to *feel* more rested each morning and feel more peaceful at night.
- I don't want to stress out about money so often.
  - I DO want to *feel* more prosperous more often.
- I don't want to be exhausted all the time.
  - I DO want to *feel* more energized.

As you engage in your process, know that it's about what you want to *feel*, not about what others want of you nor what you want of others. Right now, it's not about trying to control the situation, outcome or circumstance. With this, we can go deeper with flipping your "don't wants" on their head, and extracting what you actually *do* want to *feel*.

POINT TO PONDER #8
Exploring How I Want to Feel

I Don't Want...	*Instead, I DO Want to Feel...*

Recite and affirm at least three times today (starting now). Plug a reminder into your phone so you don't forget: "I love exploring what I really want; I'm worthy of happiness and health."

Now, let's continue the unpeeling of how you want to feel so you can begin to more deliberately experience it in your day-to-day life and not just in the far-off future.

You've deduced you want to experience certain feelings more than others. Likely, you want to experience certain feelings more because you haven't been experiencing them enough in your current life. We're going to take this exercise a step further so you can get clearer on how to experience these feelings more because you're worthy of feeling better!

As I explored more of how I wanted to feel, I didn't want to keep waiting until my next goal was accomplished to feel them. I still had goals, but I didn't have to depend on those goals to enjoy my day-to-day life. I realized if I thought I'd *feel* better by having or not having to do or deal with certain things, it was my feelings that mattered the most. I had to ask myself what I could do to experience more of what I wanted to feel on a regular basis.

Building off the aforementioned examples, all of which I've experienced at some point in my life, we can add "one way I could feel more of this is by". I illustrate below:

- **Don't Want:** To work in a toxic work environment
  - ○ **Do want:** I want to feel more fulfilled by the work I do each day.
    - ■ **One way I could feel more of this is by:** remembering why I chose this work in the first place; shifting my schedule to include more direct care throughout each day, and limiting my paperwork to specific timeframes. If needed, looking for a new work environment.
- **Don't Want:** Passive-aggressive, one-sided, or codependent relationships
  - ○ **Do want:** I want to feel supported by my relationships.
    - ■ **One way I could feel more of this is by:** asking for help when I need it or calling a friend to share how I'm feeling. Scheduling a girl's night out.
- **Don't Want:** Work stress and commitments getting in the way of quality time with my kids.
  - ○ **Do want:** I want to feel more present with my kids.
    - ■ **One way I could feel more of this is by:** Being done with work at a specific time each day and sticking with it. Scheduling specific trips or activities to do with them.
- **Don't Want:** To have to do everything exceptionally and by myself.
  - ○ **Do want:** I want to feel like I have room to breathe and relax.

- **One way I could feel more of this is by:** Doing something for and with myself before everyone wakes up or during my drive to work, like listening to my favorite radio station that makes me crack up, or making my favorite latte, yum!

- **Don't Want:** To think I look like crap in my own body every day.

  - **Do want:** I want to feel proud of my body and feel good about how I take care of it.

    - **One way I could feel more of this is by:** Eating salads for lunch, going for walks throughout the day, buying clothes I feel comfortable in.

- **Don't Want:** Restless nights.

  - **Do want:** I want to feel more rested each morning and feel more peaceful at night.

    - **One way I could feel more of this is by:** Listening to calming music before bed and staying off all electronics for at least an hour before bed.

- **Don't Want:** Money stress, especially it being an added stress to marriage.

  - **Do want:** I want to feel more prosperous and safe in discussing money with my partner.

    - **One way I could feel more of this is by:** reminding myself that all our bills have always been covered. Dedicating a specific amount of money to doing fun things with the kids each month. Having bills on autopay!

- **Don't Want:** Exhaustion.

  - **Do want:** I want to feel more energized.

    - **One way I could feel more of this is by:** drinking water at least four times per day and eating nourishing foods that taste good to me. Having the kids help me clean in a fun way so we are enjoying time together, and house stuff is still taken care of.

In the next Point to Ponder, you'll be engaging with this process yourself. It may take some time for you to work through this process, as it plays out differently for everybody. However, once it clicks, it's common to no longer feel like you're just "going through the motions." Instead, it can finally feel like living with purpose, on purpose.

POINT TO PONDER #9
Finding The Way to Feeling

It's your turn to take some time exploring what you could do to experience what you want to feel on a more consistent and deliberate basis.

- Don't Want: _____
  _____

  ○ Do Want: _____
  _____
  _____

  ■ One way I could feel more of this is by: _____
  _____
  _____
  _____

- Don't Want: _____
  _____

  ○ Do Want: _____
  _____
  _____

  ■ One way I could feel more of this is by: _____
  _____
  _____
  _____

- Don't Want: _____

  _____

  ○ Do Want: _____

  _____

  _____

  ■ One way I could feel more of this is by: _____

  _____

  _____

  _____

- Don't Want: _____

  _____

  ○ Do Want: _____

  _____

  _____

  ■ One way I could feel more of this is by: _____

  _____

  _____

  _____

- Don't Want: _____

  _____

  ○ Do Want: _____

  _____

  _____

■ One way I could feel more of this is by: _____

_____

_____

_____

• Don't Want: _____

_____

○ Do Want: _____

_____

_____

■ One way I could feel more of this is by: _____

_____

_____

_____

• Don't Want: _____

_____

○ Do Want: _____

_____

_____

■ One way I could feel more of this is by: _____

_____

_____

_____

- Don't Want: _____

_____

o Do Want: _____

_____

_____

■ One way I could feel more of this is by: _____

_____

_____

_____

Recite and affirm at least three times today (starting now). Plug a reminder into your phone so you don't forget: "I love exploring what I really want; I'm worthy of happiness and health."

In this chapter, you've more generally connected with how you want to experience your life by daydreaming differently. You later started to get more specific about what you might do to feel how you want to feel more often. That specificity will continue to bring about the added clarity you need moving forward as you seek to make confident choices and commitments to yourself. Take a moment to reflect on what you've engaged with so far, and your experiences as you've worked through this chapter.

_____

_____

_____

What was it like for you to get more specific about experiences that help create more of the emotions you want to feel?

_____

_____

_____

If I'm honest, there were times when I felt annoyed by all of this. Like, *Come on, really, this is not going to help.*

Other times I felt saddened by it, like, *Oh my goodness, this is a lot for me to have to do and sustain just to feel better! This is so much work!*

However, over time, I felt invigorated and empowered by it. Like, *Wow, it's simpler than I made it out to be. I can do this. I've already done it before, so I can do it again. It's totally doable and so worth it!*

Your experience will have its own ebbs and flows. Ultimately, no matter who you are, your experience will largely be impacted by the lens with which you view things.

BRAINS USE LENSES TO INTERPRET THE WORLD.

Our brains tend to make associations about people and things, based upon our lived experiences. Different life experiences then create different associations for different people. Simply put, the associations or categories our brains put things into, create the lens through which we perceive the world around us. Our brains continue to gather evidence from around us and filter it through the lens we are most accustomed to using. Our brains generally look for evidence that seeks to support the associations we've already been making. This unconsciously bias form of data collection about life, reinforces the same old thoughts and feelings we've experienced the most over our lifetime.

It doesn't matter if you're aware of it or not. You do unconsciously have bias lenses through which you perceive the world around you. We all do. Just like breathing and blood circulation, your brain and body do their thing whether you tell them to or not. However, when you learn to bring your attention to the lens you're using to interpret things, you gain the power to shift that lens if it needs shifting.

For example, if you wanted to, you could slow down right now and notice if your brain is filtering your thoughts and feelings about this week's core concept through a critical lens or a resourceful lens. You can do that by noticing how you're reacting right now. Is your body or face tense? Are you feeling disengaged? Are you thinking about closing this book or skipping an exercise? If so, you're likely using a more critical lens right now.

However, if you notice your body is more relaxed, your thoughts are more reflective, and you're feeling more curious, you've likely got a more resourceful lens on at the moment.

What do you notice?

_____

_____

_____

_____

_____

As you notice that, you can decide if the lens you're using is helpful or if you'd like to try a different lens.

Let's put this power into practice. In the next exercise, you're challenged to put on a lens that helps you to filter the data you've been collecting about your life, your circumstance, etc., in a more resourceful way.

To do that, you're going to put on a lens that helps you filter out the white noise of life and let in the "exceptions." The exceptions are the times in your life, past, present or even anticipated future, when you *did* or *do* experience some of the feelings you desire (which you identified in Point to Ponder #8). If you're willing to try this in an area of life that's been hard for you, then our typical lens on the subject will get activated and be challenged.

POINT TO PONDER #10
Evidence + Exceptions

It's so much easier for most people to wear a critical lens. Critical lenses focus on what isn't happening, what doesn't seem possible, and what isn't feeling good. Critical lenses are protective. Today, you'll intentionally put on a less critical and less problem-focused lens. Instead, you'll try on a more resourceful, appreciative type of lens.

Unlike the former exercise where you focused on what you could do, today, you'll focus on exceptions where what you desire to experience *has* or *is* currently being experienced in your life in some way, somehow. Here are some examples of applying a more resourceful, exception-finding lens:

- I want to feel more fulfilled by the work I do each day.

  - Yesterday, Linda wrote me a note of appreciation for changing her life in such a significant way. It felt so rewarding. I felt fulfilled and fully believe I helped enhance her life experience!

- I want to feel supported by my relationships.

  - When I asked Sarah if she'd have time to talk with me last week during my drive home, she said yes. I really loved that call. It felt so good that she made time to talk with me, and just being able to talk with her about what was going on with me felt refreshing.

- I want to feel more present with my kids.

  - I remember how happy my daughter was over the weekend when I sent edible arrangements to her for her birthday. I can't forget the smile on her face and how excited she was that she got a delivery specifically for her. I was totally enthralled in the moment, and I know my kids could feel it too. Her excitement had my full attention.

- I want to feel like I have room to breathe and relax.

  - When I pulled over after work last month and just sat in my car for a few extra minutes to meditate before getting the kids, it felt so good. I got to breathe and relax.

- I want to feel proud of my body and feel good about how I take care of it.

  - On Mondays, while my daughter is at dance and I take the boys for a walk around the neighborhood, I feel so good. I enjoy our time together, being active in a way that fits so neatly into my schedule. I feel good moving my body when I do this.

- I want to feel more rested each morning and feel more peaceful at night.
  - I used to read before bed, and I remember sleeping better on those nights.

- I want to feel more prosperous.
  - Having my bills on autopay is really helpful. I know the bills are all taken care of, and it feels comforting.

- I want to feel more energized.
  - I remember those few months last year when I had more energy. I was more conscious about what I was eating and wasn't staying up so late trying to get things done at night. I was taking Vitamin D at that time too, since my levels were low.

If you truly slow down and allow yourself to reflect, it's almost certain there are or have been times, no matter how small or subtle, when you did get to experience some of those feelings you desire. For many people, those times can be found in the present if you allow yourself to look with a different lens. If not in the present, it's okay to look to the past.

What exceptions can you find? Take time now to write those down and gather the evidence to support that you *can* see, feel, taste, and touch more of what you want both now and later.

I want to feel/experience:

Evidence of a time when I already felt this way or experienced this was:

_____

_____

_____

_____

_____

_____

_____

_____

_____

_____

_____

_____

_____

I want to feel/experience:

_____

_____

_____

Evidence of a time when I already felt this way or experienced this was:

_____

_____

_____

_____

_____

_____

_____

_____

_____

_____

_____

_____

_____

_____

_____

I want to feel/experience:

_____

_____

_____

_____

Evidence of a time when I already felt this way or experienced this was:

I want to feel/experience:

Evidence of a time when I already felt this way or experienced this was:

_____

_____

_____

_____

_____

_____

_____

_____

_____

_____

_____

I want to feel/experience:

_____

_____

_____

_____

_____

_____

Evidence of a time when I already felt this way or experienced this was:

_____

_____

_____

_____

_____

_____

_____

_____

_____

_____

_____

_____

_____

_____

_____

_____

_____

_____

Recite and affirm out loud at least three times today (starting now). Plug a reminder into your phone so you don't forget: "I love exploring what I really want; I'm worthy of happiness and health."

You really are doing great. This is not false encouragement. I've done some version of these processes myself and have helped others to do them as well. I know they take commitment. While many of these processes may seem simple, they are so incredibly powerful.

Honestly, the processes you're engaging in change lives.

Are you allowing them to begin to change yours? Are you allowing the processes to truly help you hit your RESET button?

Since you've come this far, I bet you are! Know that you're indeed worthy of the RESET you desire! You're worthy of hitting your RESET button whenever you desire because life is about living; it's not about just getting through. If you're not satisfied with how you've been living your life, why not get more intentional about how you're living it; right?

To further build upon the foundation we've begun to lay in these past few chapters; you'll need to connect with your motivators even more deeply. Those motivators are your reasons why.

You've already begun to get clear on your why by identifying the feelings you want to feel, connecting to your dreams more generally, and then getting more specific with the experiences you desire more of in your life.

However, there is a Why beneath your why, and it matters a lot.

We will call this your "Why". Most people skip over this completely, which thwarts continued progress.

The Why underneath your Why is essentially your fuel. Your life fuel. It's not only what helps you gain momentum and clarity, but (depending on what kind of Why it is) it also helps sustain momentum.

For the RESET process, we will not talk about the different types of fuel that come from different types of Whys or motivators. If you want to dive deeper into those, there are additional resources on my website, BoldAndBalancedCoaching.com.

What is important here is that you connect with the Why beneath your Why and do so with intention. You can do this by adding the word "because" to the end of your desires (using your responses from Point to Ponder #9). Some people may also find it helpful to add the "because" to the end of their "don't wants," and that's okay too. You can add your "because" to the end of multiple layers of the work you've done thus far, but it's important you end and focus on the "because" connected to your *desires* and not those associated with your "don't wants." Adding your "because" to the actions you've begun to associate with your desired experiences will further enhance the power of this exercise.

I think it's easiest to understand this process by sharing some examples. For consistency and ease of application, let's build off of the examples we've been working with thus far:

- I don't want to work in a toxic work environment *because* it drains me.
  - I want to feel more fulfilled by the work I do each day *because* I went into this field to help change lives, and I want to feel like I'm doing that.
    - Remembering why I chose this work in the first place; shifting my schedule to include more direct care throughout each day and limiting my paperwork to specific timeframes. Looking for a new work environment *because* I know that the more comfortable and supported I feel in my work environment, the better I can serve others.

- Passive-aggressive, one-sided, or codependent relationships *because* I wind up feeling angry, resentful, and alone.
  - I want to feel supported by my relationships *because* the kind of connections I have with people matter to me.
    - Asking for help when I need it or calling a friend to share how I'm feeling. Scheduling a girl's night out *because* I will feel more connected; and when I feel more connected, I enjoy my life more.

- Work stress and commitments getting in the way of quality time with my kids *because* I want to feel like I'm a good mom.
  - I want to feel more present with my kids *because* I care about how my relationship with them affects their lives.
    - Being done with work at a specific time each day and sticking with it. Scheduling specific trips or activities to do with them *because* I want to create meaningful experiences with my kids that we can all look back on with fondness, love, and gratitude.

- I don't want to have to do everything exceptionally and by myself *because* it exhausts me and makes me feel like I need to rush through life.
  - I want to feel like I have room to breathe and relax *because* I want to enjoy my life now and later.
    - Doing something for and with myself before everyone wakes up or during my drive to work—like listening to my favorite radio station that makes me crack up, or making my favorite latte, yum! *Because* these small moments with myself actually refuel me and help me be a better me.

- Think I look like crap in my own body every day *because* it feels bad; I feel guilty and kind of like I'm working against myself.
  - I want to feel proud of my body and feel good about how I take care of it *because* I want to feel supported by and at home within my own body.
    - Eating nourishing foods, going for walks throughout the day, buying clothes I feel comfortable in *because* it reminds me to love and like myself unconditionally (and helps me to model the same for my kids).

- Restless nights *because* it makes it hard to feel good and function the next day.
  - I want to feel more rested each morning and feel more peaceful at night *because* I will be able to function better the next day and feel happier.
    - Listening to calming music before bed and staying off all electronics for at least an hour before bed *because* it helps me set boundaries for myself, my health, and my own needs.

- Money stress *because* it creates stress in my marriage that puts me on edge and restricts what we can do.
  - I want to feel more prosperous *because* I feel less stressed and less mental clutter.
    - Knowing all our bills are covered, reminding myself how far I've already come, do fun things with the kids, and still having money in the bank. Having bills on autopay *because* I feel more free!

- Exhaustion *because* I'm not able to really be who and do what I really want to be and do.
  - I want to feel more energized *because* I want to have energy to do fun things!
    - Drinking water more regularly and eating nutritious foods. Having the kids help me clean in a fun way so we are enjoying time together and house stuff is still taken care of *because* I'll have more fun, be more present, and feel more like the me I want to be!

Can you feel how adding the "because" at the end of these statements helps to create deeper meaning? You may also notice, if you hadn't already, that there is a lot of repetition from exercise to exercise. Remember, this is all part of the process to rewire your brain, and thus, hit your RESET button.

Have you ever learned something new really well by doing it just once? Have you ever shifted your perspective without some kind of emotional experience leading the way?

No, you have not.

That's because it's not how our brains or bodies are designed to work. In part, you're learning how to deliberately connect with strong desires and emotions relating to the things you care about using repetition. This helps you move closer and closer toward what you want. You're using the knowledge we have about how our brains and bodies work to help you do it in a sustainable way.

It's okay if you notice a sense of frustration or annoyance about any repetition. Just know repetition is a vital part of your RESET process. If you're having a strong reaction to it, you can write about this reaction in the space below. There is no need to ignore how you feel; you just don't need it to hinder your progress with hitting your RESET button. Take a few moments to write out whatever comes up for you around the repetition and then move forward:

_____

_____

_____

_____

_____

_____

_____

_____

_____

_____

_____

_____

_____

_____

_____

_____

_____

_____

_____

As you go through this repetition process, you may start to realize some changes in what you desire. It's possible some of what you thought you really wanted, you no longer find to be very important to you. You may also find that some of what you didn't realize was important to you, now actually feels much more significant. That's another benefit of the repetition process. The more you connect with the words you're writing and the feelings you feel as you write them, the more clear you become on what you want.

POINT TO PONDER #11
Exploring the Why Beneath My Why

Let's get started with exploring the Why beneath your Why. There's no need to complete this process for every single desire you've identified thus far. You'll want to go deeper on only the desire(s) you're choosing to prioritize at this time. Do not try to shortcut your way through this process by skipping a statement from any of the important desires you choose. Remember repetition is your friend in this process.

Use your statements from your prior Points to Ponder and complete the below fill in the blanks. Again, you do not need to complete this exercise for every desire you previously outlined. At this point, if you haven't already, you can start to narrow down your focus for exercises. Only use the exercise excerpts from the desire(s) that feel strongest for you. Choosing one or two is more than sufficient, but I've left spaces for two others in the event there's a challenge with dwindling the focus down more.

You can use the examples provided in this chapter to help guide you through this process.

1. I **DON'T** want to _____

_____

_____

BECAUSE _____

_____

_____

*I **DO** want to feel* _____

_____

_____

BECAUSE _____

_____

_____

I could choose to do or focus on _____

_____

_____

BECAUSE _____

_____

_____

2. I *DON'T* want to _____

_____

_____

BECAUSE _____

_____

_____

I DO *want to feel* _____

_____

_____

BECAUSE _____

_____

_____

I could choose to do or focus on _____

_____

_____

BECAUSE _____

_____

_____

3. I **DON'T** want to _____

_____

_____

BECAUSE _____

_____

_____

*I **DO** want to feel* _____

_____

_____

BECAUSE _____

_____

_____

I could choose to do or focus on _____

_____

_____

BECAUSE _____

_____

_____

4. I **DON'T** want to _____

_____

_____

BECAUSE _____

_____

_____

*I **DO** want to feel* _____

_____

_____

BECAUSE _____

_____

_____

I could choose to do or focus on _____

_____

_____

BECAUSE _____

_____

_____

Recite and affirm out loud at least three times today (starting now). Plug a reminder into your phone so you don't forget: "It feels good to connect with what I want and why I want it. I'm worthy of connection and happiness."

What was it like to go several layers deeper and begin exploring the Why beneath your Why? Connecting what you want, don't want, and could do, to the reason you desire it helps gain a more profound clarity than most people ever realize they need. Were you at all surprised by some of your reasons Why? If you did not complete this process, go back and complete it before moving forward. Remember; each component and exercise in this book builds upon the previous one.

POINT TO PONDER #12
Highlighting What Matters

Today, you're going to take action and heighten the impact of your Why exercise. As helpful as it was for me to explore why I wanted what I wanted, I realized I didn't have the same kind of emotional connection to all my Whys. I was questioning some of my reasons. Initially, it seemed both enlightening and confusing all at the same time. I needed to better understand my Why beneath my Why, so I looked for patterns and brought my awareness back to my emotions again.

A simple but effective way to do this is to re-read what you wrote, and then highlight the parts that stick out as most meaningful to you. Below are some examples indicating what parts connected strongly with the Why beneath my Why for myself and others I've worked with. Bold lettering indicates where the highlighting would go.

- I don't want to work in a toxic work environment *because* it drains me.
  - I want to feel more fulfilled by the work I do each day *because* I went into this field to help change lives, and I want to feel like I'm doing that.
    - Remembering why I chose this work in the first place; Shifting my schedule to include more direct care throughout each day and limiting my paperwork to specific timeframes. Looking for a new work environment *because* I know that the more comfortable and supported I feel in my work environment, **the better I can serve others.**

- Passive-aggressive, one-sided, or codependent relationships *because* I wind up feeling angry, resentful, and alone.
  - I want to feel supported by my relationships *because* the kind of connections I have with people matter to me.
    - Asking for help when I need it or calling a friend to share how I'm feeling. Scheduling a girl's night out *because* I will feel more connected; and when I feel more connected, **I enjoy my life more.**

- Work stress and commitments getting in the way of quality time with my kids *because* I want to feel like I'm a good mom.
  - I want to feel more present with my kids *because* I care about how my relationship with them affects their lives.

■ Being done with work at a specific time each day and sticking with it. Scheduling specific trips or activities to do with them *because* I want to create meaningful experiences with my kids that we can all look back on with **fondness, love, and gratitude.**

- I don't want to feel like I have to do everything exceptionally and by myself *because* it exhausts me and makes me feel like I need to rush through life.

  ○ I want to feel like I have room to breathe and relax *because* I want to enjoy my life now and later.

    ■ Doing something for and with myself before everyone wakes up or during my drive to work—like listening to my favorite radio station that makes me crack up, or making my favorite latte, yum! *Because* these small moments with myself actually **refuel me and help me be a better me.**

- Think I look like crap in my own body every day *because* it feels bad; I feel guilty and kind of like I'm working against myself.

  ○ I want to feel proud of my body and feel good about how I take care of it *because* I want to feel supported by and at home within my own body.

    ■ Eating nourishing foods, going for walks throughout the day, buying clothes I feel comfortable in *because* it reminds me to **love and like myself unconditionally (and helps me to model the same for my kids).**

- Restless nights *because* it makes it hard to feel good and function the next day.

  ○ I want to feel more rested each morning and feel more peaceful at night *because* I will be able to function better the next day and feel happier.

    ■ Listening to calming music before bed and staying off all electronics for at least an hour before bed *because* it helps me set **boundaries for myself, my health, and my own needs.**

- Money stress *because* it creates stress in my marriage that puts me on edge and restricts what we can do.

  ○ I want to feel more prosperous *because* I feel less stressed and less mental clutter.

    ■ Knowing all our bills are covered, reminding myself how far I've already come, do fun things with the kids, and still having money in the bank. Having bills on autopay *because* **I feel more free!**

- Exhaustion *because* I'm not able to really be who and do what I want to be and do.
  - I want to feel more energized *because* I want to have energy to do fun things!
    - Drinking water more regularly and eating nutritious foods. Having the kids help me clean in a fun way so we are enjoying time together and house stuff is still taken care of *because* I'll **have more fun, be more present, and feel more like the me I want to be!**

Go back and read the reasons you wrote for your "because" statements. Highlight the most powerful Why statements and write those out for today's Point to Ponder.

To truly hit your RESET button, you'll need to review the highlighted Why statements. The Why beneath your Whys are your fuel. For them to fuel you, you need to be connected with them so you can *use them*!!

BONUS CHALLENGE.

Take it a step further today and put your highlighted Why list somewhere you can readily access it. You may choose to take this book with you for reference, take a picture of the page with your phone, or perhaps write it out on a piece of paper and store it in your pocket. Throughout the day, read and connect with the Whys you highlighted. Continue to connect with them throughout your RESET process. Maybe you even want to place it somewhere you can't help but see it, so you effortlessly see it throughout your day, like on your wall or in your calendar. It's up to you!

Allow yourself to be creative about this challenge and choose to intentionally connect with what you highlighted.

Recite and affirm out loud at least three times today (starting now). Plug a reminder into your phone so you don't forget: "It feels good to connect with what I want and why I want it. I'm worthy of connection and happiness."

CHAPTER RECAP

In the first chapter, you spent time getting more specific about what you don't want because when you're clearer on what you don't want, you can get clearer on what you do want.

You've used your "don't wants" to identify what you *do* want to feel and experience. You started general and then got more specific, so you could enhance both your clarity and awareness, boosting motivation to move forward in a direction that feels better for you so you can hit your RESET button. You practiced using your imagination and you also highlighted the reasons Why this RESET journey is so important for you.

When you're clearer about what you really want to feel and experience, you become more motivated and better equipped to take action that helps move you in the direction you desire! That is why you've spent significant time sorting and sifting to identify what you *do* want and how you want to *feel*. You've boosted your motivation and gained greater clarity. Throughout your RESET, you will continue to consider the changes you do want and the shifts you do desire to experience. You'll continue to go deeper, get clearer, and ultimately experience greater fulfillment and a sense of freedom as a result.

Go you!

This chapter is such a powerful one, so if you need to dive into it again, it's okay. Do it. You can take some time to review the chapters, your notes or even go back and redo the whole process from the week if you need or want to.

Will you focus on your list of "don't wants," or will you focus on the feelings you *do* want and some of the ways you can create those experiences in your life sooner rather than later? Don't get me wrong, we all need a variety of experiences in life and some of the contrasting moments that our "don't wants" offer up to us at times. We don't, however, need to live constantly focused on the thoughts and feelings that keep re-fueling them.

Now, sit back, relax, grab something yummy or comforting and reflect on the insights you've gleaned thus far in your process. You've got this.

CHAPTER INSIGHTS

Use these questions to reflect and capture insights from this chapter.

Have I been accustomed to focusing more on what I don't want or what I do want?

_____

_____

_____

_____

Was it hard to raise my awareness and move through this chapter's core concept, or was it not so difficult for me? What was it like? How would I describe it?

_____

_____

_____

_____

_____

_____

_____

Did I feel any resistance? Why or why not? Did I gain any clarity on this?

_____

_____

_____

_____

What will I choose to focus on today? This week? Why?

_____

_____

_____

_____

You've covered a lot so far. You've examined what you're sick and tired of, what does not fit anymore, and what boundaries you're either missing or need to build up. You also began to daydream more about what your RESET would look and feel like. You've gained clarity about what you do and don't want, which has helped you feel more motivated to hit your RESET button.

Recite and affirm out loud at least three times today (starting now). Plug a reminder into your phone so you don't forget: "It feels good to connect with what I want and why I want it. I'm worthy of connection and happiness."

*Supplemental resources available to dive deeper into motivation are available at BoldandBalancedCoaching.com, such as Motivation & Time Creation, The Mini Course. Resources and offerings may vary over time.

Chapter Four:

Core Concept Three: Beliefs and Being

Beliefs are not facts, but they are often treated as such. This chapter will take you on an exploration of certain beliefs that have wreaked havoc on your life and can easily stall out your RESET. Core concept three challenges you to go deep. Yes, even deeper than where we've gone so far.

To RESET in any area of your life, you'll have to do or view some things differently than you have before. It's part of the change process. To do things differently, you have to shift the internal processes that have kept you where you've been. In order to shift these inner workings, you have to become more aware of what they are. You'll notice that self-awareness is a crucial practice throughout the course of this book (as need be the case for any good self and life-optimization book).

There's a lot of increased awareness required throughout this process. You've already begun to increase your awareness of your desires and feelings. You've gotten clear on what you don't want, you've gotten clearer on what you do want to experience more of in your life, and you've gained more clarity about why all of this is important to you at a personal level.

You've conquered massively important components of your RESET process!

Congratulations!

After I got clear on what I didn't want, what I did want, and why I wanted differently, it was time to get even more real with myself—and in this chapter, you'll be doing the same.

You'll be asking yourself the same challenging questions I had to ask myself:

Am I really being the person I want to be?

Am I being the person I need to be to experience more of what I want?

Are you?

On the surface, these questions may not seem too deep, but by this point, you know we're going way beyond the surface level here. This next step requires exploration and a better understanding of your beliefs and your way of being. Because it's one thing to know what you do and don't want and why, but it's a whole other thing to regularly *show up* in a way that helps create the kind of experience you want in your day-to-day life.

For example, say you want to experience more peace, ease, and connection with friends, family, or colleagues. But, when you interact with them you're quick to ramp up the defense system or jump to judgment. This means something is amiss. The reactive pattern of immediate defense or jumping to judgment means you're not contributing to creating more of the peace, ease, and connection experience you desire more of. Consider it. When in an actively reactive state, are you simultaneously feeling connected with ease or peace? It's unlikely.

I wanted to experience more peace, ease and connection. Before my RESET experience, there had been many nights when I struggled to sleep. I'd lay there feeling angry and anxious. I'd wake up feeling angry and anxious. But the performance I put on for the world was one of poise and confidence. My inside world and my outside world didn't match. I didn't feel the peace, ease and connection I desired.

I distinctly remember one morning, back in 2014, when I woke up to take a shower. I stepped in, looking forward to the warmth of the water and privacy of the showers walls. It was one of the only two places I could escape (the other one being my car). But, as I ran my hands through my hair, a clump of my hair fell out. I looked at it in my hand. I couldn't believe it. *Was this from stress? No. Not me. I couldn't possibly be that affected by stress.* I was the one who always "had it together" because, well, I always believed I had to be.

Thinning and missing hair.

Poor sleep.

Chronic fatigue.

And yet I was still piling more on my plate and refusing to ask for help.

I wish I could say that I learned my lesson after that incident, but I did not. The stress continued to pile up, and I continued to believe I had to sacrifice myself for quite some time before I'd intentionally begin my RESET process.

It was a few years later that I really started asking myself if I was honestly being the person I wanted to be to create the difference I wanted to create in my life. This was not an easy question to peel back the layers on. It was hard. It meant taking an incredibly deep look at myself. That included examining my choices and behaviors and my attitude, what I was saying and choosing not to say, and the boundaries I was unnecessarily putting up plus the ones I needed to put up but hadn't been.

Why did I take so much on all the time? Was I really being the me I wanted to be, or was I being who I thought I *needed* to or *should* be? Was I trying to prove something to myself? Was I trying to prove something about myself?

I wanted to feel more fulfilled, energized, supported, and grateful, but I was always putting on a face like everything was okay. I acted as if I could handle it all on my own, all the time. Could my "I got it" attitude and behavior lead me to create the life experiences I wanted more of in the long run?

Well:

If I never let on when I needed a break . . .

If I was always stretching myself and my schedule . . .

If I was never asking for help and staying guarded about my vulnerabilities and needs . . .

If this was how I was showing up, was I really being a cooperative contributor to the life I wanted to create and enjoy?

Crap! Crap! Crap!

I wasn't.

I wasn't being a cooperative component of my desired life experience, at least not in a sustainable, intentional, feel-good type of way.

I was working hard by taking a lot of action, but I was not super clear on how to just *be*. To be the me who not just wanted more support, ease, and connection but the me who *allowed* more support, ease, and connection into my life experience.

I was only able to realize this because I got willing to dig into some of my patterned ways of being and the beliefs that had kept me living that way for so long. In this chapter, you'll begin your own "Beliefs and Being" dig by getting curious about how you view yourself, how you want to view yourself, and where your day-to-day actions toward yourself and others align.

We will start with how you're being and then move into your underlying beliefs.

POINT TO PONDER #13
How Am I Generally "Being"?

To get started with a better understanding of how you're being, you'll want to get a baseline of how you would describe yourself *now*. Using five to ten adjectives, describe how you're showing up in your day-to-day life, generally speaking. Be very honest with yourself.

For example: *Caring. Hardworking. Independent. Strong. Capable. Responsible. Reliable. Compassionate.*

1.

2.

3.

4.

5.

6.

7.

8.

9.

10.

Now, go back and look at your list of five to ten descriptive words. Respond honestly to the below questions:

Do these ways of being align with how I *want* to show up in my life right now? In other words, does how I'm showing up match how I actually want to show up in my life?

_____

_____

_____

_____

_____

Is acting this way helping me to create more of the experiences I desire in my life? In other words, is the way I'm showing up making me feel good about being me?

_____

_____

_____

_____

_____

Are any of the ways I'm showing up backfiring or creating additional barriers? In other words, is my general attitude and behavior working against me in some ways?

_____

_____

_____

_____

_____

Great. In the first part of this exercise, you focused more on how you're generally being. Now it's time to get more specific. In this next part of the same exercise, think only of how you're showing up with regard to the specific RESET you're wanting to prioritize right now. For example, if I looked at my list of desires from prior exercises, I may choose to focus my priority RESET on experiencing more peace, ease, and connection in my relationships. I'd keep this priority RESET in mind when completing the below section. It's okay if you're having trouble narrowing down your priority RESET. RESET desires generally fall into some kind of category, like relationships, health, wealth or happiness. Revisit your desires until you can distill your desired RESET down to one or two you'd like to prioritize for now.

Priority RESET (example): To experience more peace, ease, and connection in my relationships

Write your priority RESET below. Try to stick with one, but if it's too close of a tie, do two:

Priority RESET 1:

Priority RESET 2:

PART II: GETTING MORE SPECIFIC

As you think about the priority RESET above, ask yourself:

How would I describe how I am currently, or how I most often am showing up in this area? What adjectives might fit me here? How might I describe the way I'm acting or reacting and the attitude or outlook I tend to have about this area(s)?

You may find it helpful to use this list of comparisons for reference as you get curious about how you're currently showing up in this area(s) related to your priority RESET: Doubtful or hopeful? Pessimistic or optimistic? Guarded or open? Unsure or confident? Worried or sure-footed? Anxious or secure? Scared or content? Hardcore or go with the flow? Alone or supported? Annoyed or understanding? Loving or spiteful? Angry or happy? Resentful or grateful? Gracious or judgmental?

1.

2.

3.

4.

5.

6.

7.

8.

9.

10.

Now, go back and look at your list of descriptive words. After reviewing them, respond honestly to these questions about the area(s) you're wanting to RESET. Don't overthink your answers but try to be true to yourself with your responses.

Is how I've been showing up aligning with how I *want* to show up for my RESET? Does how I'm showing up in this area of my life match how I actually want to show up in this area of my life?

Has acting this way been moving me closer to my desired RESET, further away, or keeping me stagnant? In other words, do I feel good about how I'm showing up in this area of my life?

Have any of the ways I've been showing up been backfiring or creating additional barriers? Have my attitude and actions been working against me and my desired RESET?

_____

_____

_____

_____

_____

_____

_____

BONUS CHALLENGE.

Take mental note of how you show up throughout the day. After observing your attitude, decisions, and behaviors (your way of being) today, come back to this next question.

Ask yourself: Is how I'm being helping me to experience more of what I desire to experience, or is it having a different kind of impact? The impact I notice it having on my RESET currently is…

_____

_____

_____

_____

_____

Recite and affirm out loud at least three times today (starting now). Plug a reminder into your phone so you don't forget: "My mind is fascinating and wants to cooperate. I'm excited to experience what's next!"

Alright, you have your list of ways you would describe yourself both generally and with your RESET. You also have some notes as to whether those ways are helpful or not so helpful in creating more of what you desire to experience in your life. Keep your list handy (preferably, you're writing in this book or have a notebook or folder dedicated specifically to your RESET, so it's all readily available to you when needed). You'll be referencing this list in upcoming exercises.

The tricky thing about noticing how we are being is that some thoughts and beliefs fuel them, which we often are not aware of. Research has shown us time and time again that our thoughts impact how we feel, and how we feel impacts how we behave. Thoughts we keep thinking, whether we realize we're repetitively thinking them or not, will form beliefs. Our beliefs then inform how we view ourselves and the world around us and affect our decisions and way of being.

When I checked in with how I was being, I noticed that in some areas of my life, I was being a certain way simply to avoid feeling wrong, rejected, or judged. How I was showing up day-to-day was being informed by fear. Even though I didn't realize it, I acted in certain ways because of a hidden belief (like being super independent all the time) that relying on someone else would end up with me getting hurt, betrayed or rejected.

As I leaned in more, I noticed there were broader patterns in my life that were leading a lot of my choices. As someone who prided themselves on being independent, capable, and in control, I didn't like coming to the realization that my behavior was being so significantly impacted by things I wasn't even aware of. Once I chose to acknowledge my fear and frustration, I could allow myself to feel how I felt while still slowing down enough to look under the proverbial hood. When I looked under the hood at my hidden beliefs, I found I was making many choices to avoid being rejected or because I believed I needed to prove certain judgments, stereotypes, or criticisms of me wrong. I didn't want to get hurt and I didn't want to be perceived as the "bad", "difficult", "annoying", "know it all" or "wrong" one.

Because these hidden beliefs were based in fear, I found they'd gone rigid in many ways. A rigid belief is one that views things to be a certain way and is not flexible to other ways of seeing things. It's all or nothing, black or white-type of thinking. It's typically operating in the background, like a blindspot that we're unaware is limiting our vantage point. Essentially, rigid beliefs are like small, narrow lenses resistant to any change or re-focusing.

Noticing rigid beliefs was hard. Really hard. But, it did make sense. When our brains and bodies are in stress mode, they stimulate the parts of our nervous system that focus on survival. Survival is an all-or-nothing type of framework. You either survive, or you don't. It's simply more efficient for our brains to function in this black or white (rigid) frame of reference under distress because efficiency is of vital importance when needing to survive. The trouble with this is that our brains and bodies are so often stressed nowadays that they use a rigid type of framework more often than is helpful or necessary.

In other words, people's brains and bodies are living in survival mode so often it's become their daily default. And, they don't even realize it.

Unfortunately, I see these hidden rigid beliefs pop up for people all the time, and I was no exception. I always considered myself a pretty open person, but I'd developed some rigid beliefs about my identity. These rigid beliefs about myself prevented me from being the *me* that allowed my behavior to contribute to more of the life experience I wanted for my RESET.

For instance, I believed I needed to be a strong, independent woman who helps others. At first glance, that sounds great—admirable even, doesn't it? But I'd developed a hidden belief that being a strong, independent woman who helps others meant I was *not* allowed to be a person who shows weakness. It meant I was *not* allowed to be a person who relies on others. I was *not* allowed to ask for help or let others help me. The gray middle ground, where I could be both a woman who helps and a woman who receives help, was missing.

The gray middle ground goes out the window when our brains and bodies are in stress mode. Most of us live in stress mode more often than our human bodies were intended to (and more often than our human minds care to admit). That means most of us struggle with some rigid beliefs whether we want to admit it or not, but we are so accustomed to this way of thinking and being, that we don't even realize it's creating barriers for us.

My well-intentioned desire to be a strong, independent, helpful woman had internally turned into a very guarded and stressed-out version of me. As nuanced as this may seem, it was significantly impacting my relationships and mental health. I thought, *I'm on my own. I've got no one to rely on.* Sometimes I'd catch myself, eyes glazed over, just staring at nothing-ness and wondering what the heck I was really doing with my life. Stoic, I'd look in the mirror. I didn't recognize myself.

How about you?

Are there certain ways you're being that, at the surface level, seem well-intentioned, but when you go deeper and observe the hidden belief beneath it, you notice there is a fear there?

Perhaps something feels different, off, or not aligned?

How is it influencing how you're really being?

Here's an illustration to show one of a few common ways this may play out for some high achieving individuals:

Bob had done well in school. He excelled in all of his academics. He learned that performing well got him praise, rewards and positive attention. Overtime, he began to only get positive attention, rewards and praise when he excelled. Anything less than excellence basically resulted in Bob feeling rejected and like a failure.

Bob grew up labeled as a "smart", "high achieving" and "successful" person. Over the course of his childhood, those labels turned into expectations. As Bob strived to achieve those expectations, they turned into beliefs about how he *had* to perform in the world. This expected way of performing turned into his default way of being. Although unintentionally, his childhood labels were internalized and turned into a sense of his adult identity and assessment of worth. The pressure to always perform with excellence or otherwise risk failure or rejection, led him to pursue high-stress jobs that wreaked havoc on his mental health. The sacrifice and hard work was constantly justified, because that way of being "successful" had unconsciously become an ingrained belief about how he needed to show up.

Labels and expectations, like the ones Bob was ascribed and internalized, get certain ways of being attached to them. Some people then come to believe they must always "be" that way. When that way of being gets turned into a hidden belief and goes rigid, the person may fear *not* always showing up as the smart, high achieving, or successful person. Therefore, any mistake they make or challenge they face feels like a threat to who they are. This creates a lot of internal pressure, and we can see it manifest with things like perfectionism, high anxiety, or people-pleasing tendencies. The rigid belief is they must always "be" this certain way, without exception or grace, *or else.*

A rigid framework for how you should be, ultimately results in challenges like resentment, burnout, rage, depression, relationship issues, and even physical ailments like headaches, etc.

Over time, I discovered all types of beliefs about myself, my life, and my relationships with others—beliefs that startled, annoyed, and bothered me or caught my attention in some way. I realized they needed to be identified for me to address them.

You'll need to identify a hidden belief before you can address it. We all have hidden beliefs. We all have beliefs that go rigid. We just don't all take the time to discover and tend to them. Without identifying how you're being and what beliefs are connected with that way of being, you can't do much about it. While the exact beliefs and ways they impact your way of being are unique to you, the truth that they do exist and they do indeed influence one another, is true for us all.

During the exploration of my beliefs and how I was being, I had to ask myself things like:

How am I showing up in my day-to-day life? (Which you began to do in the former exercise.)

How am I showing up for myself?

How am I showing up with my colleagues, partner, kids, friends, family, and others?

Am I okay with this?

Are you?

Are you okay with how you're showing up?

POINT TO PONDER #14

Am I Okay with How I'm "Being?"

This next exercise is going to ask you to get even more specific about how you're being. While how you show up in one area of your life likely overlaps with how you're showing up in another area of your life, there's often differences among the two which need to be sorted out. For example, you may act much more patient at work, but much less patient at home. The differences in how you're being won't show up as much when you stay general, so getting more specific about how you're showing up in various areas of your life will provide you with more detailed data you can use as you move forward with next steps.

Based on your preliminary observations and reflections from the previous "being" exercise, ask yourself:

Am I okay with how I'm showing up for/how I'm being towards:

My colleagues?

My partner?

My kids?

_____

_____

_____

_____

_____

_____

My friends?

_____

_____

_____

_____

_____

_____

My family?

_____

_____

_____

_____

_____

_____

_____

Someone or something else?

_____

_____

_____

_____

_____

_____

Am I okay with how I'm showing up for myself and how I'm being towards myself?

_____

_____

_____

_____

_____

_____

Is it possible, in some ways, I may be fearful of *not* showing up in a certain way? Why or why not?

_____

_____

_____

_____

_____

Recite and affirm out loud at least three times today (starting now). Plug a reminder into your phone so you don't forget: "My mind is fascinating and wants to cooperate. I'm excited to experience what's next!"

If you're honestly engaging with each Point to Ponder, you're doing great. This process is more like a marathon, than like a sprint. So, do not rush yourself through it. The intentional application and engagement with the processes throughout this book are more important than the time it takes to complete any one exercise. This chapter is challenging, but challenge means you're growing, so consider this an amazing growth opportunity!

When you explore how you're being within your relationships, you can begin to more deeply question **why** you tend to be a certain way. Asking this why question helps connect you to some of the beliefs that have contributed to you being that way, whether you've realized it or not.

In the former Point to Ponder, you started to get curious about potential fears associated with how you're being in various relationships. Relationships are important. Since we are a social species, we experience things relationally. Relational experiences extend beyond other people. You have a relationship with yourself, food, nature, your home environment, your work environment, and even material things, like your car and money. Therefore, even if your RESET didn't seem to have anything to do with a relationship in the traditional sense, there is a relational experience you'll need to dive into to hit your RESET button effectively.

Beyond a shadow of a doubt, your beliefs influence your way of being (aka, how you tend to operate and the mood you tend to experience). The previous sections started you exploring some of your very own hidden beliefs that've been influencing your behavior in the background. Now, let's continue to expand on those hidden beliefs.

As we grow, we have different experiences with different people. We learn more about ourselves and the world around us based upon our perception of those experiences. Our perceptions help us create our sense of identity within this world. They help us figure out how to navigate our communities and relationships, keep ourselves protected, and figure out what direction we do or do not want to go in. Our experiences influence our perceptions, and our perceptions influence how we experience things. In tandem, these lead us to think things about ourselves. We learn and interpret how we *should* be.

Consider some of the *shoulds* or *should nots* that come to mind for you as an ending to these sentences:

I should be more like . . .

I shouldn't want . . .

I should look more . . .

I should be able to . . .

I shouldn't feel . . .

I should be . . .

I shouldn't be . . .

Shoulds are often used to dictate what to do and how to be. They can be framed in many different ways, like what is *expected* of us or what we *must* do. No one is exempt from receiving and perceiving messages about how they should or shouldn't be. It's what we do with those messages that makes the biggest impact. Did we internalize them and therefore believe they must dictate a part of who we are? Did we question them and allow them to be separate from ourselves and our identities? Did we push hard against them and therefore keep them as a negative focal point we constantly work to repel?

Shoulds become super harmful and toxic when they are internalized over time. You may have heard me say it before (and I will say it a million times again), when we "should" ourselves too much, it creates shame. Shame does not serve us. It hurts us. Therefore, I call them the "shameful shoulds," and I encourage you to pay attention when you hear the word "should" being used. See if there's any shameful messaging or experience tied in beneath it, either hidden or overt.

I shared earlier in this chapter about some of my shoulds. I believed I *should* be strong, independent, hardworking, and helpful to others. I believed it well into my young adulthood. It was what a good, successful woman *should* do.

I deeply believed that was how I should be, especially if I wanted to prove stereotypes and nay-sayers about me wrong.

It was how I *should* be if I wanted to be good, accepted, or liked.

It was how I *should* be if I wanted to be successful.

It was how I *should* be if I were to be of value, professionally or otherwise.

Yet, I had lived my life for decades, having no idea those shoulds were fueling my choices.

The shame fueled by my shoulds led me to develop a very rigid idea about how I *should* be. Those kinds of *shoulds* tend to create the hidden fear connected with hidden beliefs. The shoulds get tied to an "all or nothing" type of thinking. They tend to create that rigid, black or white framework for thinking about and understanding things.

Let's use me as an example. If I *should* be a particular way to qualify as a good, successful woman, than behaving any other way (like setting my own boundaries, slowing down, or asking for help) meant I was *not* being a good, successful woman. There was only one or the other. There was little to no gray area or wiggle room, mess-ups, or imperfection. Although hidden from my understanding for decades, that rigid perspective impacted how I *believed* I *should be* and, therefore, affected how I was showing up in my life. It influenced my beliefs about myself; it influenced how I felt and behaved, too. It influenced my definition of self—my very identity.

Your beliefs, especially the hidden ones, impact *how* and *who* you're *being*.

Today, you'll check in to see what some of your hidden beliefs may be and venture to bring forth one or two of them to the surface so you can become more aware of them. You'll begin getting curious about who you believe you *should* or *should not* be and how that may be impacting your life and your desires.

Here's another example often experienced by busy professionals, students, parents and leaders alike. You desire more quality time with loved ones, but you believe you *should* be a hard worker.

If your hidden belief about what it means to be a hard worker is to always be available no matter the hour and to relentlessly persevere, then this belief about how you *should* be is impacting the time you set aside for quality personal interaction, leisure and rest. When rigidly applied, this belief asserts that anything other than that rigid version of being *hardworking* is considered lazy (other terms some may have had thrown at them in place of lazy could be *bum, mooch, failure, disappointment, good for nothing*, not a *man or woman, dispensable*, etc.). With this rigid, hidden belief operating in the background, saying no, taking time off, or setting work/life boundaries are all considered the opposite of being a hard worker.

To avoid feeling lazy or unproductive, you keep working longer hours rather than setting time boundaries. You may gain benefits at work by being that way. You may have a great reputation professionally or be considered a powerhouse of a leader. However, you may also feel exhausted, sick, resentful, or unappreciated. That ongoing behavior will continue to impact your quality personal time with loved ones. It will wind up affecting not only how you're feeling day to day (mentally, emotionally, and physically) but also how your relationships are going. It's unlikely any positive change will happen if this hidden belief isn't addressed.

Although it may seem small, your hidden belief impacts how you're *being* in a big way. In turn, how you feel, live, and even show love are affected, too.

A similar example can be found in the guilt many moms feel when taking on the belief that they *should* be able to do everything for everyone without flaw, failure, or tending to their own personal needs. When this belief is held rigidly, moms feel stuck. It's impossible to consistently achieve that way of *being*, so the pressure to do so can and does often result in resentment, depression, overwhelm, anger, guilt, shame, and other challenging feelings.

Another common experience I've seen with high achievers, caretakers and leaders is the belief they must always be the responsible one. If this applies to you, then you may hold the hidden belief that you *should* always be able to get everything done exceptionally well or with impeccable promptness. Therefore, any behavior that doesn't align with the rigid definition of responsible equates to something like *unreliable* or *not good enough*. Feeling that way often results in feeling rejected, judged, or unaccepted in some way. To avoid feeling bad, you may overwork to fulfill that rigid definition of "responsible". However, because the definition of how you *should* be as a responsible person is (silently) rigid, it prevents you from experiencing the better quality of health and relationships you desire. You likely feel stressed and fatigued quite often.

None of this means it's bad to want to be a responsible or hard-working person. The challenge occurs when the underlying belief about how you should or should not be, is applied too rigidly, too often. You can replace the term *should* with *must* or *supposed to* and produce the same or similar results.

The above are just a few common examples; there are many others. You may relate strongly to those examples, or they may have led you to think of a completely different set of hidden beliefs and ways of being that resonate with you specifically. Notice whichever your experience is. Neither is wrong.

POINT TO PONDER #15

The "Shoulds" and "Should nots" of "Being"

Are you showing up and *being* more because it's how you desire to be or because it's how you believe you *should* or *should not* be? In the space provided below, brain dump whatever has come up for you as you engaged with this chapter thus far. It may be helpful to use this prompt to get started:

Have I been most concerned about being who I *should* be, who I *shouldn't* be or being *who I want to be?*

Recite and affirm out loud at least three times today (starting now). Plug a reminder into your phone so you don't forget: "My mind is fascinating and wants to cooperate. I'm excited to experience what's next!"

Beliefs based on fear often feel strong and relentless. The way to address them is to become aware of them so you can move through them, better understand them, and ultimately shift them. Unchecked beliefs will influence your way of being, whether you intend them to or not. I know it can feel like a lot to take in, and perhaps you're skeptical about all of this. That's fair. Most people do not mentally and emotionally excavate themselves the way you are in this book. It takes courage. It takes you being bold and honest in a different way than you've ever been before. It would probably feel easier and more comfortable to just stop right here, put the book down, and call it a day. After all, you've done a lot already. Right?

The truth is, I can't tell you exactly what will come up for you in the remainder of these pages. I can't tell you it'll be easy or go smoothly. I can only tell you that you were attracted to this book for a reason. You made it this far for a reason. You've stayed curious and engaged in this book for a reason. I happen to believe the primary reason is you're ready for some change which will ultimately better your life experience and help you be a happier, healthier version of yourself. This RESET process helps people do just that, in their own personalized way.

If you'd like to feel and see even deeper shifts, then press on. Continuing to explore particular beliefs that are informing your way of being is an integral part of the process and that's where we are headed next.

POINT TO PONDER #16
Identifying "Should-Filled" Messages

You've got your mind more open to your hidden beliefs by getting curious about your *shoulds* and *should nots*. Now, let's go deeper. For the next exercises, you'll need your notes from Points to Ponder #13-14. You'll be referencing them throughout this next exercise.

Step 1. Review your reflections in the Points to Ponder exercises from this chapter so far. Especially, review notes like your descriptive word list in Point to Ponder #13 and how you've been showing up toward others in Point to Ponder #14.

Step 2. Choose the one or two words that describe your way of being, which you feel most strongly about "needing to be". These two words are the ones you feel most strongly you *should, must,* are *supposed to,* or feel *pressured* to be. They are likely the ones that come up for you the most in your day-to-day life, like feeling pressured to be perfect, productive, or always reliable. If it feels stronger for you to focus on what you *should not, must not,* or *aren't supposed to,* it's okay to write those out too.

Examples:

I should be hardworking.

I should always be willing to give.

I should be able to figure everything out on my own.

I should be strong.

I should excel.

I should be giving because I shouldn't be selfish.

I must not fail.

I shouldn't want because I should just be grateful for what I have.

Step 3. Write the two you chose in the space below:

Descriptive Word/Statement 1:

Descriptive Word/Statement 2:

_____

_____

_____

_____

_____

Step 4. Write out any thoughts or reactions coming up as you consider the experiences and messages that have taught you to be these particular ways. Connect the words or statements you chose to any rigid definitions of what it means or looks like for you. I've provided prompts to help you get started. Take your time with it. You may need to come back to this exercise multiple times because more thoughts will flow in once you begin to explore them. Don't limit yourself to the prompts provided. In your own words, continue to challenge yourself to remain aware of and write out any thoughts coming up as you engage with this process.

Examples of thoughts and messaging that may have gotten paired with *shoulds* or *should nots*:

I should be hardworking: I have to be hardworking, or people will think I'm lazy. If I'm lazy, I'll never get anything done, and then I'll be a failure, low life, disappointment, just like [insert name of person you want to avoid being like]. I can't be a disappointment. No one likes a disappointment. I need to be liked.

I should be willing to always give: If I'm not doing something for someone else, I'm not really being useful. If I'm not being useful, I'm not really fulfilling a purpose. What's the point of life if I don't have a purpose? I have to always be giving to other people and not be selfish, or I'm not living life right. I can't be selfish. Selfish is bad. I have to be good.

I should be able to figure everything out on my own: If I can't figure things out, I'm a mess. I always had to keep it together when I was a kid because it seemed like my whole family was a mess. I had to be the one to keep it together because no one else was going to do it. I remember one time I asked for help with something small, and I got blasted. There is no place for me to have needs or to mess up. I have to keep it together and rely on myself, or my whole world will fall apart. If everything falls apart, it'd be my fault. I can't handle that.

I should be strong: Showing emotions is a weakness, and I can't afford to be weak. I have to be strong, or I'll be weak and vulnerable. I won't ever let myself be weak and vulnerable because I can't get hurt again. They'll just try to use or take advantage of me. I can't trust anyone. People always betray or disappoint me, so I need to be strong and not let anyone know how I feel. It's not safe to trust other people. I'll just get hurt again. Being alone is safest.

I should excel: I remember growing up, I was always told I had to work hard to get what I want and to be successful. So, I did. And even though some things came easy to me, other things were hard, so I pushed myself hard to do them. It felt like the only way I could get any real recognition was if I excelled. Any mess up would make me a disappointment. I have to excel, or I'm just not good enough; I'm a failure. People won't like me.

Some prompts you could use are:

I think I should be _____ because

_____.

If I'm not acting like _____ I

have worries or fears that _____ may happen.

I have to show up as _____ or else

_____.

I'm expected to be _____,

or _____ will be disappointed.

If I'm not _____,
then I'm not good enough/useful/of value.

The *shoulds* or rigid beliefs you've unveiled have served as hidden motivators for your decisions and behaviors over the years. Were there *shoulds* that felt stronger, more confusing, or less powerful for you than others? Were there certain descriptive words you found hard to connect to a *should*?

REFLECT BELOW:

What thoughts, experiences, messages, or fears arise?

Recite and affirm out loud at least three times today (starting now). Plug a reminder into your phone so you don't forget: "My mind is fascinating and wants to cooperate. I'm excited to experience what's next!"

No matter what your experience was, it's a good start, and it's okay. Remember, this is all a process. If any of this is feeling too much for you, be sure to take breaks, and if needed, seek professional help. There is no shame in gaining support when and where we need it. We are a social species for a reason. We don't just yearn for support and connection; we need it. We benefit greatly from it.

Unveiling your *shoulds*, rigidity, and hidden beliefs can help you see what's been motivating some of your life choices with more clarity. If the *should* feels especially strong, there may be a deeper or long-held fear attached to it. Those strong *shoulds* are often hard to see because they feel so true and familiar. They are often tied to either trauma or childhood experiences because of how amenable our brains and bodies are during such times. If this is the case for you, be gentle with yourself along this discovery process. It's possible to be gentle and still be honest.

Now that you're more aware of rigid hidden beliefs, you probably don't want how you're *being* and *believing* to be operating from a place of fear, right? Most of us would prefer there to be some feel-good and fun leading the way instead.

While fear is a normal and necessary human emotion, it's certainly not where we want to live our lives or operate from on a chronic basis. You're now more aware of some of the fears operating in the background of your psyche and how they impact your life. With this awareness, you can begin to get more intentional about changing them up a bit!

A main fear of mine was rejection. One of the ways I was being was guarded because I was afraid of not *being* perceived as a good, successful woman. I did not want to live in a place where I was *being* a certain way simply because I feared rejection. I wanted to help when, if, and because it felt good. I wanted to be strong and still be able to have my own feelings felt and needs heard. I wanted to be independent and still trust and rely upon others in my close circle. Very deeply, I wanted to be less guarded, so I could be more of the me that felt good and had fun.

But, the responsibilities of my life took precedence over taking care of myself: motherhood, managing finances, full time work, navigating newlywed life while simultaneously taking care of our home, pumping for the baby, and attending grad school. Every time I added a responsibility my guard would amp up due to my own hidden beliefs and fears (unbeknownst to me at the time, of course) around others not wanting to be there for me. I'd think things like:

They don't really get it.

They wouldn't want to help me anyway.

I can do it myself, I don't need to bother anyone.

They'll think I need them or I can't handle it on my own.

They'll just say I did this to myself. I can handle it.

The big and scary stuff hiding behind rigid beliefs and ways of being can easily overtake our ability to see and connect with the good, fun, and the present. When we call out the big and scary stuff for what it is, we are in a better position to assess if it's truly something to be scared of in the moment or not. If it's not, we become free to bring our attention to things that feel good, more fun, and more present. When we can engage with ourselves, others, and our lives in this way, things tend to feel and look better than they did.

Since I was living in the throes of busy-ness, I wasn't fully living. I made little to no time for fun. *What busy working mom has time for fun when there's always so much to get done?* I'd catch myself using phrases like this to justify the days of mental haze. But fun is an important part of life, and living devoid of any fun, humor or laughter results in unfulfilled living. It wore me down before. I wouldn't let it wear me down again.

My hyper-focus on being an independent and responsible working mom led me to forget about some of the ways I could have fun and feel good. Despite my fears, there had been areas of my life where I had allowed myself to let my guard down a bit and be free at certain times. If I really thought about it, there had been some times when I'd allowed myself to have fun and just do something because it felt good. In retrospect, those times were few and far between, but they did exist. I just needed to reconnect with those experiences and what they felt like.

Slowly and intentionally, I introduced more fun experiences into my life. I'd take a bit more time in the car by myself so I could sing out loud before going to work. I'd silly dance with my kids, or listen to a radio station that made me laugh. If I'm honest, introducing more fun into my life didn't come easily to me. I had made myself the responsible, goal-achieving, always-got-it-together one. If I'm being even more honest, I continue to learn and practice new ways of introducing fun into various areas of my life to this day. I'll still catch myself from getting caught up in the "get it done" mentality and remind myself to make time for fun. The difference now is that I get sucked in less frequently, so I have fun more often. When I do get sucked in, it lasts for a shorter duration and it doesn't rule me or my life. Fun is no longer tertiary; I recognize it as a primary focal point of my life.

If you want to sustainably hit your RESET button, some fun, feel-good stuff has to be incorporated into how you're *being*. It's not enough to just do something that seems fun; you'll need to engage with things that truly *feel* fun to you, and do so with a light-hearted perspective and attitude. Be open to be silly, let loose, and release the need for control even if just for bits of moments at a time. To do this, we will need to explore what makes you laugh, smile, or feel energized in some positive way. I'll offer some examples of what I unveiled for myself as well as others I've worked with.

For me: living room dance parties with my kids, dancing silly by myself, singing and dancing in the shower, painting or drawing, listening to music from my teen years, baking and cooking just because, rough housing with our dog.

As I engaged (and continue to engage) more with these fun and feel-good activities, I also experience more of the ease and connection I wanted to experience with myself and my loved ones.

Others have shared: gardening, creating or listening to music, creative writing, reading, high-impact activities or sports (i.e., skydiving, running, hiking, soccer), playing games with kids, creative arts, choreography, and wood-making, to name a few.

POINT TO PONDER #17
Feeling For the Fun

The power of intentionally engaging in fun activities and doing things that feel good is sorely under-estimated. Brains and bodies chronically under stress, will gain a much needed respite when engaging in fun, feel-good experiences. Keep this in mind as you respond to each question openly, honestly, and thoughtfully.

Are there areas in my life where I allow myself to be more relaxed?

Are there areas in my life where I do things that feel good to me?

_____

_____

_____

_____

_____

_____

_____

_____

_____

Are there times when I do allow myself to have fun for the sake of fun?

_____

_____

_____

_____

_____

_____

_____

_____

_____

Are there things I'd like to do that I think would feel-good or fun? What ideas do I have about this that are inspired from the past, seem like present opportunities, or I'd consider as potential for the future?

Take some time today to write out those experiences and notice how you feel while you do so. Then, get curious. Might you be able and willing to incorporate pieces of any of these fun, feel-good experiences into your daily life more often? Would you incorporate any within your week this week? Have *fun* with this! Really allow yourself to connect with feeling a fun, relaxed, or energized state of *being*. Write or draw it out.

If it's hard to connect to any of this right now, pause and take a day to consider, observe and reflect. You may start by simply looking around to notice what peaks your interest. You may choose to look back over your life and connect with times that felt fun or energizing for you in the past. Perhaps view pictures of times you remember having fun before, to get yourself connected. Then, come back to this exercise, read the prompts and try again.

Recite and affirm out loud at least three times today (starting now). Plug a reminder into your phone so you don't forget: "My mind is fascinating and wants to cooperate. I'm excited to experience what's next!"

TAKING ACTION.

Okay, you've compiled a few ideas of things you can do to help you step more into a fun, relaxed, or energized way of being from a feel-good (not forced or fake) place. Now, it's time to take action!

Choose one of the fun, feel-good ideas you connected with in the prior Point to Ponder. Use it to inspire one thing you could do *today* that allows you to feel good or have fun. Schedule at least ten minutes to do this today. Not because you *should*, but because you *choose* (and deserve) to be someone who creates opportunities to feel good more often. Then, take a moment to connect this feel-good experience with your desired RESET experience.

Even if you can't do the exact thing you've written down in your notes, you can use it as a starting point. Just get curious about what it was about the thing that led you to feel the way you desired to feel. For example, say you want to feel more energized and you remembered feeling energized back when you used to coach your child's soccer team. However your kids are all grown, and there are no soccer teams to coach. What do you do? You can start by asking yourself: *What was it about coaching soccer that invigorated me so much? The laughter of the kids? The adrenaline of running around the field?* Investigate what helped energize you and incorporate that!

If it was running around the field, then go for a run, visit a local soccer field, or kick a ball around for a bit. If it was the laughter of kids, perhaps you give a grandchild, niece, nephew, or other young child in the family a call and talk for a few fun moments. It's able to be figured out as long as you're willing to get resourceful; think outside the box. Prioritize connecting with a state of feeling good so you can begin to reinforce a belief that you're allowed to *choose* to feel good about the life you're creating for yourself.

CHAPTER RECAP

How did this deep dive of a week go for you? Did you take time to notice some beliefs you have carried around about how you *should* be and why? Were you able to identify any areas where you were thinking too rigidly? Did you allow yourself to begin to connect with ways of *being* that feel good to you? Did you allow yourself to connect with ways of being that feel more aligned with what you desire to experience more of in your life? Did you commit non-negotiable time for creating and enjoying an experience that allowed you to feel more of it? Are you moving closer to the belief: *I can create more of the experiences I desire to have in my life!*

"Beliefs and Being" is an important area to become aware of because it's about how we live in our own lives. It's where the power comes from to enhance our life experience for the better. Please know, however, this is an ever-evolving process. It's not a one-and-done deal.

You may continue to discover some hidden beliefs today or tomorrow, and as you do, you will become more and more equipped to address them. Day after day, month after month, year after year, decade after decade, you will become better at identifying them and shifting them to serve you better. The self-development process never ends, and there is no shame in being an ever-evolving human. I'm still learning more about myself each and every day. I expect I will continue to do so as long as I'm physically alive on this earth.

CHAPTER INSIGHTS

One of the fears I held was: if I wasn't focusing on taking as much action as possible, then I'd become less productive and therefore less needed and less valuable. If I were less productive, I'd risk being viewed as not good enough; this thought process was fed by fears of failure and rejection. I worked to shift my definition of productivity to being less rigid so that it wasn't so tied to a fear of rejection or failure. Ultimately, I reshaped my beliefs about what it meant for me to *be* a productive, successful, independent woman.

This week, did I allow myself to explore my way of being and some of the hidden beliefs beneath those particular ways of being?

Am I okay with what I've become more aware of this week? Why or why not?

Am I choosing to more intentionally be the me who chooses to create the felt experiences I desire more of (think feel good, fun, energized, etc.)?

_____

_____

_____

_____

_____

_____

_____

_____

_____

This chapter is a deep dive chapter. It can be one where folks need extra time to review the lessons, revisit their notes, and further reflect on what has been discussed and explored. Take the time to do that this week. Allow yourself to review anything that seems foggy or needs more of your attention. Spend time writing it out or rereading any sections you need.

You're amazing for staying committed to your RESET process this far! Keep it up!

Recite and affirm out loud at least three times today (starting now). Plug a reminder into your phone so you don't forget: "My mind is fascinating and wants to cooperate. I'm excited to experience what's next!"

Chapter Five:

Core Concept Four: Choice and Intentionality
(A deeper connection to beliefs and being)

This is a pivotal week in your RESET journey, but first, stop and take a pause. Take a moment to pay attention to the fact you're still here engaging in this process. You've committed. You've learned. You've grown. You've developed some new perspectives or gained insights necessary for you to get to this point. You have much to credit yourself for. No one else could have done this for you.

Often, I find myself reminding both therapy and coaching clients they are the ones who've chosen to stick with their commitment to their self-enhancement and healing journey, so they are the ones who get the credit. Don't gloss over the efforts and time you have put in so far. You're doing well. You deserve credit for how far you've come. Pause now. With whatever form of self-congratulation fits for you, give yourself the credit you're due before continuing.

Did you pause and take time to celebrate the efforts and time you've put in? If the answer is no, then take time to do that now. If the answer is yes, then good! We can continue.

Last week, you got curious about how you were being in your life and explored some of the hidden beliefs holding you down in those ways of being. By unveiling some hidden beliefs, you've enhanced your awareness. This awareness process allows you to get more intentional about how you're being and *why* you're choosing to show up that way. While the awareness process is uncomfortable, it's an essential part of hitting your proverbial RESET button.

After unveiling some of my mental cobwebs, I realized I needed to still get even more clear on and committed to who I truly wanted to be. My RESET was no longer about trying to control or fix things to be the way I wanted them to be in my life—it had become about me and how I wanted to be within my life. Looking under the hood at some of how I was being and why, helped me to realize many things. For one, the only way I'd effectively be able to change some of the hidden beliefs and scared parts within me, was if I decided how I wanted to be and why I wanted to be that way, regardless of challenging life circumstances. In some ways it sounded simple, and in other ways it sounded unrealistic. Regardless, simple and easy are not the same, and I'd become living proof that the boundaries of "unrealistic" could be pushed much further than I'd previously believed.

So, do you know how you want to be?

Do you know how you want to show up?

Do you know what kind of human you value being? Are you really clear on this?

I had to choose, intentionally, how I wanted to show up and be in my life, even more deliberately than I thought I had been. You, too, will be faced with the opportunity to decide how you truly want to be within your life.

Maybe you're okay with how you're *being*, but you're not okay with *Why* you're being that way. If this is the case, it's time to redefine Why you're *being* the way you're *being* and create a new and improved reason for Why you *choose* to show up *being* that way.

This chapter guides you to get more intentional about how you choose to show up in your life and for your RESET. Whether you're not okay with certain ways you're being or you're not okay with certain reasons why you're being that way, you'll need to learn how to do some more internal shifting. You'll need to explore what you want to shift to and why you want to shift in that direction. This intentional way of being is where core values come in. Deliberately exploring my core values stands as a pivotal point in my journey.

As I grew throughout my RESET process, I realized I valued trust but didn't really trust anyone. I valued service but did not let people serve me. I valued compassion but showed little compassion toward myself. I valued forgiveness but I struggled to forgive myself and others. I valued open and honest communication, but I wasn't open and honest with the people I was closest to in life. I wasn't paying attention to what I valued, and, therefore, I wasn't showing up in alignment with how I truly valued *being*.

I began to get curious about what I valued. I'm not referring to the tangibles I valued (like money, house, car, or tech) nor what I socially valued (like reputation or martyrdom). I'm talking about what I genuinely valued about my life and how I wanted to show up within it. That exploration shaped the version of me that I wanted to align with.

Once I had my core values delineated, they served as a reference point for me, even (and especially) when life had twists, turns, or trauma.

I had to identify my core values.

I had to stop looking at my circumstances to decide how I should be or how I should react.

I had to stop allowing my fears to decide how I should be or react.

I had to get clear on what it looked like for me to demonstrate my core values and then commit to consistently connecting with them *on purpose*.

To do all of this takes intentional choice. It doesn't just happen to you or for you. Getting clear on your core values and showing up in alignment with them takes ongoing, consistent, and intentional action.

I had to ask myself repetitively:

Who do I want to be?

How do I want to be?

Why do I want to be that way?

What would it look like for me to show up that way right now?

What's getting in my way of showing up the way I want to be?

What strengths do I have that I can use to help me move through those barriers?

Am I committed to molding myself into that enhanced version of me?

Why? What do I stand to gain? How would it change the way I feel about myself? My life? My relationships?

This chapter is pivotal in your RESET process because you *decide* who and how you're committed to *being* starting now and moving forward. Doing so will allow you to feel more fulfilled, aligned, and able to enjoy more of your life *now* (not just later).

This chapter isn't about how you should be because of your current circumstances or the cards you happen to be dealt in life. Regardless of what your RESET goal has focused on so far, this chapter isn't about how you need to be to achieve one particular tangible goal either. You carry yourself with you no matter what goal you've got and no matter what place, or time you're in within your life. Therefore, this chapter is about how you value yourself as being and intentionally choosing to be that version of yourself, both in your RESET focus and your life as a whole. It's about setting yourself up to live a life of integrity.

POINT TO PONDER #18
Observe

Today, observe. Observe yourself. Observe how you're *being*. Notice how you're *being* throughout your day. Notice how you're *being* toward yourself, family, coworkers, strangers, drivers on the road, friends, and so on. If you like what you notice, smile and allow yourself to feel good about how you're showing up each time you notice. If you don't like what you notice, simply take a mental note, and ask yourself how you'd like to show up instead. Don't beat yourself up throughout this observation phase. Just notice, and then get curious about the potential values underlying how you really want to *be*.

No need to write today; simply observe and become more aware of how you value being.

FROM OBSERVATION TO EXPLORATION.

I didn't want a superficial RESET. I wanted something legitimate that'd impact me and my life for the better, for the long haul. That is what the RESET process allowed me to do, using the same processes I'm walking you through in this book. You're moving closer to knowing and claiming who and how you desire, choose, and value *being*. You're more aware of how you thought you should be and that this does not need to be what drives who you are and how you show up. You also took the time to become more aware of how you want to *be*, which leads you to the next explorative portion of your journey.

Surprisingly, the next part I want to share with you is one of the most influential parts of my RESET journey. It's what helped me over the hump from wondering if this process was worth my continued efforts to feeling and deeply believing my life was changing in a significant way from the inside out.

I shifted into making a conscious effort to no longer have my life be led by who I should be or what goal I needed to achieve to prove something. My life had become more about *me* aligning with *me* and *being* that me on purpose, with purpose. Cue the corny music, I know. It sounds fluffy, cliché, and perhaps too good to be true. However, this part of my process continues to be one I incorporate into my life to this very day. It's one I discuss with all my clients at some point because of how helpful it is when incorporated properly.

This next piece is so effective because it can serve as an anchor during the smooth times and the hard. We all need something we can quickly, easily, and powerfully connect with during turbulent times. Because when things get hard, we need a guidance system we can lean on. If that guidance is too gray and undefined, it's hard to understand and anchor into.

This anchor is your core values.

Sometimes, it can be hard to figure out how we value being because we get so wrapped up in how we should be based upon societal or childhood messages. Good thing you already did some digging into your shoulds. Your work will pay off here because you'll have more of an awareness about how you value *being* now than you would have before. To break down the exploration of what your core values are, we are going to start with how you value *being* in the various roles of your life. It won't exactly tell you your core values right off the bat, but it will give you a good gauge for where to start.

For example, as a mom, I thought I should value selflessness, but it burned me out. Instead, I realized I valued being present and patient. By being a present and patient mom, I'd be better able to support my kids, and I'd be able to enjoy my time with them more. We'd be able to have more fun together. Experiencing these kinds of connections with my kids was one of the desires I identified wanting to experience more of, way back at the beginning of my RESET journey.

How about you?

I invite you to get familiar with this next part of the process because, if nothing else, it will help you connect with *you* better. Exploring and connecting with your core values helps you get even more intentional about choosing how you want to *be* so you can RESET at that level of yourself.

To do that, you need to explore how you want and value *being* in a deeper way. It's often easier to dig into how we value *being* by first thinking of how we value *being* within the roles we fill each day.

POINT TO PONDER #19
A Self-VALUE-ation

Take time to ask yourself how you value being within the context of the roles you fill each day and write down your responses. Indicate why you value showing up in these particular ways. I've offered common roles below to get you started, but feel free to use and add whatever roles best suit you.

Ask yourself: "How do I value being within these roles? Why?"

As a mom or dad, I value being _____

_____

_____

_____

_____

As an uncle or aunt, I value being _____

_____

_____

_____

_____

As a grandparent or godparent, I value being _____

_____

_____

_____

_____

As a sibling, I value being _____

_____

_____

_____

_____

As a friend, I value being _____

_____

_____

_____

_____

As a partner, I value being _____

_____

_____

_____

_____

As a professional, I value being _____

_____

_____

_____

_____

As a leader, I value being _____

_____

_____

_____

_____

As a citizen or community member, I value being _____

_____

_____

_____

_____

As _____ (other) I value being _____

_____

_____

_____

_____

As _____ (other) I value being _____

_____

_____

_____

_____

Recite and affirm out loud at least three times today (starting now). Plug a reminder into your phone so you don't forget: "I know I'm well along my way. I need not know it all or be perfect to enjoy my growth. I'm forever learning and evolving."

By breaking down the values core to your way of *being*, they can become a succinct anchor that can serve as a guide for you, even when times get tough. Your core values are not about what you value in society; they are about who and how you value yourself as *being* at your very core as an individual regardless of circumstance. If your core value is compassion, then when things get tough, you practice compassion for yourself and others. It's not a fair-weather friend; it's an anchored part of who you are.

POINT TO PONDER #20
Creating The Anchor

To begin creating your internal anchor today, you'll review the provided core value terms and intentionally choose which ones stand out to you the most. Below are step-by-step directions to guide you through this process.

1. Read the list of values terms below.
2. Review your notes from the last few Points to Ponder in chapter 4 and the first two you completed in chapter 5 so far.

Connection	Courage	Forgiveness
Mindful	Spontaneity	Integrity
Peace	Structure	Helping Others/Service
Community	Cooperation	Fulfillment/Purpose
Stability	Presence	Impact
Wellness	Equity	Appreciation
Trust	Self-Expression	Wisdom
Intimacy	Flow	Creativity
Balance	Growing/ Growth	Gratitude
Humor	Challenge	Innovation
Affection	Adventure	Teaching
Joy	Independence	Harmony
Play	Consistency	Relationships
Choice/Freedom	Empathy	Learning
Recreation	Security	Communication
Kindness	Safety	Contribution
Sharing	Dignity	Knowledge
Consideration	Discovery	Faith
Authenticity	Acceptance	Healing
Effectiveness	Exploration	Awareness
Hope	Expansion	Self-efficacy
Honesty	Compassion	Inspiration

3. Scan the list of values terms again and look for connections between what you wrote in your Points to Ponder, and the below list. Notice which terms stand out to you the most.

4. Write down the top ten values that stand out to you as being core to how you want to show up within your life.

5. Look to see if any of the top ten you chose overlap with one another; then distill your core values down to your top five.

LIST OF VALUES TERMS:

MY TOP 10:

1.

2.

3.

4.

5.

6.

7.

8.

9.

10.

Next, review your top 10 and identify which ones overlap with others; collapse these like-terms together. Identify which remaining values are most strongly aligned with how you want to be as a person. Write the subsequent top 5 below.

MY TOP 5:

1.

2.

3.

4.

5.

Recite and affirm out loud at least three times today (starting now). Plug a reminder into your phone so you don't forget: "I know I'm well along my way. I need not know it all or be perfect to enjoy my growth. I'm forever learning and evolving."

To reinforce the power of your core values, you'll need to connect with why these particular values are so significant to you. You may notice your reasons Why matter a lot! That's a consistent pattern you'll find repeated throughout all aspects of any effective self-development work. This deeper level of Why serves as more than motivation; it serves as inspiration. Inspiration is much more powerful than motivation; that's really where the power is at!

POINT TO PONDER #21

Getting to the Core of Core Values

Using the list of your top five core values, write out *why* each of them matters to you and how you show up with them. For example, I value being compassionate. I value being compassionate because it helps me feel connected to myself and other people in a meaningful way. It also feels more positive and enriching than being non-compassionate. One way I practice showing up as a compassionate person is by giving the benefit of the doubt, and choosing to forgive rather than hold grudges. I know that no one is perfect, so I don't expect them to be.

Now it's your turn. The basic set-up for this exercise is: I value being [insert top core value here], because [write the reason(s) why you value being this way]. One way I practice this core value is by [identify at least one way you're showing up in alignment with this core value in your life presently].

I value being _____ because _____

_____

_____

_____

One way I show up demonstrating this value is _____

_____

_____

I value being _____ because _____

_____

_____

_____

One way I show up demonstrating this value is _____

_____

_____

I value being _____ because _____

_____

_____

_____

One way I show up demonstrating this value is _____

_____

_____

I value being _____ because _____

_____

_____

_____

One way I show up demonstrating this value is _____

_____

_____

I value being _____ because _____

_____

_____

_____

One way I show up demonstrating this value is _____

_____

_____

Recite and affirm out loud at least three times today (starting now). Plug a reminder into your phone so you don't forget: "I know I'm well along my way. I need not know it all or be perfect to enjoy my growth. I'm forever learning and evolving."

I'll be honest; it took me some time to figure out which core values really fit best for me. I tried different terms with similar meanings many times. Over the years, my understanding of those core value definitions shifted. So, the terms I use to describe my core values have shifted over time, too. The goal here isn't to "get it right". The purpose of this core values exercise is to help you get clear on who you choose to be in a profoundly meaningful way. The power of this goes beyond words and certainly extends well beyond any constricting definition of who you are based upon what society or others in your life think about you.

Now that you've written out your top five core values, it's time to put them to the test! To do so, you'll practice applying them when things are hard. During the storms of life, the lack of an anchor is most noticed, and remember, those core values serve as an anchor. The captain of a ship who is out to sea will want to know where the anchor is and how to use it before an urgent storm hits! To practice allowing your core values to be an anchor for you in your life, you'll need to practice how to apply them to your way of showing up, both when things are going smoothly and when the going gets tough.

I remember getting really frustrated with my partner because things weren't getting done around the house the way I thought they needed to. I became irritable. Rather than communicating clearly, I felt annoyed and became passive-aggressive. Of course, this was not the most efficient way to resolve the situation. Passive-aggressive behavior only muddies the water of communication more. When it came to my core values, what was most notable about my behavior was I wasn't practicing forgiveness or compassion within my marriage when relying on passive-aggressive actions to communicate my frustrations and needs.

I had jumped straight to old habits of being guarded and skipped right over showing up in alignment with how I wanted to *be*. During the frustration, I learned to practice catching myself. I reminded myself of my commitment to honoring how I want to show up by connecting with my core values. I started checking in with my core values before making any further moves or comments when I felt the frustration brew. It took some practice, but it turned out connecting with my core values could completely recenter me! I was better able to resolve the conflict with my partner and tend to the situation in a way that created much more ease, which was exactly what I wanted more of!

My core values served as an anchor for me to tap into and use as a guide for how I wanted to navigate the situation, even during a challenge. By getting more intentional in the moment, I started to realize I had more choices about how I could show up even if stressed or frustrated.

There will always be challenges in life. Life will have some kind of stressor at some point. The goal is not to eliminate all stressors in life. Instead, the aim is to more deliberately choose how you'll show up amidst those stressful times. Practicing this greatly influences your life experience and satisfaction.

To be better equipped for anchoring into your core values when challenges happen, it's helpful to practice and prepare ahead of time. Consider barriers that may occur and where you might anticipate having a hard time tapping into your core values. These are usually associated with situations, topics, or with the people you tend to feel a strong reaction to. Maybe for you, that's in your marriage like it was for me. Or, perhaps it's with friendships, at work, with your kids or in-laws, or is more contextual, like when discussing politics or injustices. The truth of the matter is circumstances won't always be ideal, but you'll still have the choice on how to show up. The more connected to your core values you are when you show up, the better you can navigate challenges with both intentionality and choice.

POINT TO PONDER #22

Applying Core Values

Ask yourself these questions and write down your responses. Be sure to take your time and be honest with yourself in your answering:

How might I apply my core values in a tough situation I'm going through?

What might make it hard to apply my core values in this situation?

How could I practice my core values even though it might be hard to do so? Is there something I could do or say to remind myself about using my core values as an anchor?

Recite and affirm out loud at least three times today (starting now). Plug a reminder into your phone so you don't forget: "I know I'm well along my way. I need not know it all nor be perfect to enjoy my growth. I'm forever learning and evolving."

YOUR STRENGTHS.

Navigating barriers, stressors, and challenges in life is something we all have to do at some point, and we can always get better at doing it. We all have strengths. Our strengths can help make this process less difficult. As you learn to anchor into your core values, it's important to remember you already have innate strengths, talents and gifts. The assets you already possess can be used to help you through challenges that arise during your RESET journey too.

I had the strength of perspective-taking. Skilled at helping bridge gaps in communication, I'd aided in connecting folks with seemingly disparate perspectives to a common goal. This strength came in handy within the toxic work environments when tensions ran high among colleagues. I was great at applying this skill in professional settings with clients and colleagues, but I hadn't realized how much I neglected using this strength to create more ease in communication within my marriage.

When we feel strongly about a certain topic, relationship, or situation, it's because it matters to us. When our emotions are amped up about things that matter a lot to us, it's difficult to access the more reasoning-based areas of our brains to help us slow down and think. As a result, we can get into a pattern of not applying the very strengths that could help us navigate the challenge more effectively. Taking the time to assess your strengths and how you could apply them in challenging areas now, will help you to think more clearly about them later. As a result, you'll be more prepared for the next time a particular challenge presents itself to you. Strengths serve as great supporters for our core values!

How about you?

What are your strengths? Humor? Organization? Problem-solving? Hospitality?

POINT TO PONDER #23
Highlight My Strengths

A Strengths-based perspective is a holistic approach taught in various settings to professionals like social workers, therapists, and other leaders. Individuals have different and multiple skills, knowledge, and experience. Getting clear and focusing on how to apply your strengths is not about being boastful; it's empowering and demonstrates respect for yourself. It will help you to be more resourceful, resilient, and confident.

Ask yourself these questions and honestly respond:

As an individual what strengths do I have? What is it I'm good at or can bring to the table in a powerful way?

How could I use these strengths to help me navigate challenges and connect with my core values more easily?

Am I using my strengths in challenging areas already? Can I use them more or differently? Are there other personal strengths, gifts or talents that I haven't tapped into yet?

Recite and affirm out loud at least three times today (starting now). Plug a reminder into your phone so you don't forget: "I know I'm well along my way. I need not know it all or be perfect to enjoy my growth. I'm forever learning and evolving."

CHAPTER RECAP

In this chapter, you created and connected with your internal anchor which you can rely upon to guide how you intentionally navigate life. As you come to know and practice using your anchor, you'll gain greater clarity and confidence in yourself. As a result, you may shift the original values terms you identified within this chapter. That's okay; this means you're growing. It's part of the process of deliberately choosing who and how you want to show up *being* in this life you are living.

You get to choose who and how you value *being*. No one else can do it for you. The power is yours! Don't give it away to anyone else.

Choose to intentionally show up this week as who and how you want to *be*, even (and especially) if a stressor, challenge, or barrier arises. Notice what this experience was like for you and take note of it in the chapter insights section.

CHAPTER INSIGHTS

Am I committed to molding myself into an enhanced version of me?

Why? What do I stand to gain? How would that change the way I feel about myself? My life? My relationships?

_____

_____

_____

_____

_____

_____

_____

_____

_____

_____

_____

_____

_____

_____

_____

_____

_____

_____

Other reflections:

_____

_____

_____

_____

_____

_____

_____

_____

_____

_____

_____

_____

_____

_____

_____

_____

_____

Recite and affirm out loud at least three times today (starting now). Plug a reminder into your phone so you don't forget: "I know I'm well along my way. I need not know it all or be perfect to enjoy my growth. I'm forever learning and evolving."

** If you need to go even deeper into understanding the beliefs and ways of being that underlie communication or interaction challenges within your relationships, courses like the Bust & Build Beliefs Bundle can help and can be found at www.BoldAndBalancedCoaching.com.

Chapter Six:

Core Concept Five: Accountability, Inside and Out

Congratulations, you're closer than you've ever been to understanding how you truly value being, and you've stayed fully committed to your RESET process. Continue to remind yourself: *No one else can do this for me.* You're well on your way to your RESET. Stay committed; you're worth it, and so are the benefits that'll continue to happen for you!

There's such amazing power in this RESET process, and it's something that can be deeply felt, isn't it?

Realizing how I truly valued being and who I wanted to become more of, drastically changed my internal experience with myself. I didn't just look confident, I felt it. My internal dialogue was less and less self-critical and more and more self-supportive.

It's okay if they don't understand. They don't have to.

I don't have to prove anything, I know who I am.

I'm compassionate. I choose compassion.

I'm grateful. I choose gratitude.

I'm loving. I choose love.

I'd repeat statements like this to myself often, and they didn't feel fake, they felt true. I was hooked. Of course, as we change our inside life, our outside life changes as well. Yet, we can go even deeper here. I was ready to put all of what I'd learned into motion in my outside life even more.

After I really anchored into my core values, things became clear to me in a different way than ever before. I started to make more choices that, to some, seemed different or risky. To me, though, those choices felt aligned. They were more purposeful for me and my desired life path than I had previously realized. The choices along this path led me to make changes at home and at work. Some of these changes felt bigger than others, but they were all relevant to my RESET (even if I didn't realize it at the time).

Still, after each big shift or big decision I made, I'd notice some old patterns popping up. At first, it felt discouraging and super annoying. After all I'd put into feeling better and improving my life, there were still things I needed to deal with?! I'd be lying if I didn't say I'd sometimes think, *Doesn't this improvement thing ever end?!*

The "improvement thing," in fact, does not have an end. Consider the first cell phone you ever had. When you got it, it was probably regarded as one of the best. However, years later, that once groundbreaking cell phone model is deemed outdated. The newer models have surpassed the old versions. Each time a new model comes out, it's an improvement based upon experience gleaned from the former one.

Improving does not need to mean anything was bad or wrong with the prior models. Each one had its place, and each one made way for new improvements to unfold over time, too. As discouraging as it can feel to have old patterns, challenges, or beliefs pop up, the fact that self-improvement doesn't end is actually a good thing. It means you do not have to stay stuck in anything. You can update yourself and reap the benefits over the course of time, just like cell phones and their systems can get updated so you don't have to stay stuck with an old outdated one that doesn't function well. There is always room to grow.

Indeed, old patterns popping up is normal. Your awareness it's happening often means you're on that different path you'd been asking for. It's human to have old ways of thinking or old patterns of dealing with things pop up during times of stress or transition. It's how our brains work.

According to Hebb's Law, "what fires together, wires together" in the brain. Basically this means the most practiced ways of being and doing become habits for your brain. When in stress mode, the brain goes for the most efficient and most well-known pathways. Your brain and body respond on autopilot like default programs. So, it makes sense your old, most practiced patterns (which got wired in as default mode) pop back up when stress or transition happens in your life. In fact, it's for this reason that your awareness throughout this process matters so much. The more you're aware of old patterns, the quicker you can catch them when they arise. The quicker you catch them, the sooner you can intervene and respond differently. The quicker and more often you intervene and respond differently, the more you are helping pathways (or habits) to wire and fire differently within yourself.

For example, when certain stressors arose in my life, I'd notice the urge to pull back from others and try to do everything on my own again. The uber-duper-super-independent woman part of me wanted to re-emerge and take control! Because I was aware of my hidden beliefs and had taken time to tend to them, I noticed what was happening. Only with this awareness could I intentionally intervene, anchor into my core values, and choose differently. Doing so helped me decide how I wanted to manage the stressors and show up as the me I wanted to be. It was a sort of internal accountability system I'd created.

Guess what? You've begun creating your very own internal accountability system too!

The more I used my internal accountability system, the more I was able to remind myself it's okay to ask for help and to take a break when needed. Whatever you'll need to remind yourself about here, will be unique to you. The internal accountability system you're creating will help you to do so.

Throughout this internal checks and balances process, I realized how important it was to be held accountable to my process and my learnings on an ongoing basis. It wasn't enough to just do it now and then expect a forever change. Accountability would help me to stick with it and, therefore, enjoy ongoing benefits.

Some people tend to rely more heavily on external accountability and support, while others, like myself, tend to rely more heavily on internal accountability and support. Both are needed. While internal accountability and support are foundational, the best way to enhance its power and effectiveness is when you've got accountability systems set-up both inside of you and outside of you. That way, if one is struggling, you've still got the other one to help. This understanding is what helped me ask for and accept outside help without all the guilt.

Eventually, my accountability revelation led me to invest in therapy. I'd gone to therapy before, but this time, I invested differently. I invested not because I had to but because I understood its value, and I wanted to. I understood my choice to invest time, money, and attention in therapy provided me with the accountability and support I needed and wanted to continue my self-enhancement journey during a crucial period in my life.

From there, I learned it was okay to invest in other forms of help, like paying for help cleaning the house. Later down the line, I invested thousands of dollars in a coach. I would never have previously made any of those investments, which is why I formerly lacked external accountability and support. Asking for help, let alone paying for it, was something that felt like a threat to my super independence before. I had also previously worried about facing other people's judgment or disapproval about how I was choosing to invest in myself and my life.

Ultimately, the investments I chose to make were well worth the money and time spent. No longer did spending money on support seem like such a burden, unnecessary luxury, or waste. It was reframed as an investment in me, my life, my dream, my health, and my family. After all, aren't those the reasons why we all want to thrive anyway?

Fast-forward several years to today as I'm writing the pages of this book. I can reflect on these past investments in support and accountability for myself with such great gratitude. The appreciation I feel for how much I've gained by allowing myself to receive from others runs so deep. I wouldn't go back and change any of it, even the ones that didn't turn out exactly how I hoped they would.

You've already demonstrated that you know your quality of life and your wellness matter by investing time, money, and attention into this RESET process. To further support this journey for yourself, you'll need accountability on the inside and the outside, on an ongoing basis. The type of accountability you need will shift over time; but the right accountability will help you to better manage your time, commitments, relationships, mental health, physical health, work-life, and so forth.

POINT TO PONDER #24

Accepting Accountability and Support

You've spent the bulk of your RESET process so far focusing on how you can internally shift and support yourself. As a result of the internal support and accountability you've been building, you get to experience external benefits. While your internal support and accountability are foundational, external accountability and support provide a helpful and powerful buffer. Let's check in on your external accountability and support systems to see where they are.

Have I been willing to accept accountability or support on the inside and the outside? What does this even mean to me?

Reflecting on yesterday, this past week and this past month, were there times when I internally experienced accountability and support from myself? How so? Did it feel good to me? Was it actually effective? If not, why not?

Reflecting on yesterday (or this past week or month—whatever works best for you), are there times when *I asked* for external accountability and support that felt good and effective for me? If so, what were they? If not, why not?

If I'm being totally open and honest with myself about my receptiveness to accountability and support within my life right now, this is what I notice as I check in with myself while moving throughout my day today…

_____

_____

_____

_____

_____

_____

_____

_____

_____

_____

_____

_____

_____

_____

Recite and affirm out loud at least three times today (starting now). Plug a reminder into your phone so you don't forget: "I'm valuable and am committed to myself and my health."

WHAT THE BRAIN HAS TO SAY ABOUT LETTING GO.

For a long time, I thought holding myself accountable basically meant being hard on myself and not letting myself "get away" with settling or any form of laziness. If I said I'd do something, I held myself to it. I didn't want to let myself "off the hook", so to speak. Ironically, I learned I was setting myself up for hardship with this tough as nails mentality. The harder I was on myself, the worse I felt. No matter what I'd held myself accountable to, it wasn't enough. That's because the brain doesn't get more focused and productive under massive amounts of self-criticism and chronic stress. In fact, it does the opposite.

We often convince ourselves that punishing ourselves, depriving ourselves, or being hard on ourselves will help us be better. But what brain science tells us is that being too hard on ourselves too often actually backfires. Instead of feeling more accomplished, we just wind up feeling like we aren't good enough and like we *should* be doing more.

That is why part of my inner-accountability work was to allow myself to take some breaks. Internal accountability isn't about being too strict or rigid with yourself. Holding yourself accountable means accepting responsibility for your actions and then choosing to respond in alignment with your own core values. If you over-extend yourself like I often did, part of holding yourself accountable requires appropriately supporting yourself to *stop* doing. It means honoring yourself by taking the break your body and brain need in order to replenish.

Although I continued to have some work to do on shifting how I held myself internally accountable, I felt even more uncomfortable accepting external support and accountability. I struggled with it because, to me, it meant trusting other people and letting them in. Being vulnerable and open in that way hadn't gone very well for me in the past, so I resisted the chance to try again. However, if you remember back to part of what I desired to experience in my initial RESET, it was connection and trust. I'd have to figure out this external accountability thing if I was going to hit my RESET button. As I gave it a try, I felt vulnerable and skeptical, but over time I was also pleasantly surprised!

At some point along my RESET journey, I realized asking for and accepting help provided additional pockets of respite for me. I gained perspective through hearing others' stories, and more opportunities for enhanced fulfillment grew through new connections. Shared wisdom of others touched me in ways I hadn't expected, and I started to experience some of the many benefits that community has to offer. This all happened through various means of external accountability, such as groups, memberships, online communities, mentors, and more.

The return on my investment in external accountability sources was and remains to be incalculable. Its return on investment lives on via my day-to-day experiences impacted by changes I make because of knowledge and insight gleaned. All those benefits aided me in my continued journey of renewed health and wellness for myself, my life, and my relationships with loved ones.

I could go on and on about the potential benefits of external accountability and support investments, but I won't because each of us will have our own unique experiences here. What matters here is that you have an openness to asking for and accepting accountability and support in various forms, both internally and externally.

POINT TO PONDER #25
Accountability Check Point

Get curious about the areas of your life where you could benefit from additional accountability or support. Is it surrounding challenges with effective communication, your relationship with food, time management, organization, parenting, sleep routine, self-confidence, managing anger, guilt, or resentment? Perhaps you're like me and have a history of struggling with super-independence to a fault?

Who and what you need to help yourself stay accountable to your RESET and ongoing development will be unique to you. Getting honest about the areas you'd benefit from receiving accountability and support in is *not* about harshly criticizing yourself and your faults. You have strengths and so do others. You have areas of challenge and so do others. Allowing others to support you in areas of challenge is mutually beneficial and is part of why we all have a variety of different strengths and challenges.

Respond openly and honestly to these questions:

What area(s) of my life am I struggling with the most right now? How so?

What evidence do I have to demonstrate these areas are indeed a struggle right now? (i.e., what ways is it currently impacting my mood or behavior, my health, my relationships, or my work?)

Have I clearly and consistently requested for or been open to receiving external support or accountability in any of these areas?

We are a social species. We need one another. We are supposed to support one another. External accountability systems are a social form of checks and balances we can use to our benefit if we do so intentionally. These external sources of support and accountability can't take the place of internal systems, but they can complement them.

Recite and affirm out loud at least three times today (starting now). Plug a reminder into your phone so you don't forget: "I'm valuable and am committed to myself and my health."

RECEIVING SUPPORT AND ACCOUNTABILITY BEYOND YOURSELF.

Anchoring into your core values and using your strengths are both vital to your RESET and overall life satisfaction, but they are not intended to be the *only* support system you have. We are a social species that, at our very core, requires connection, safety, and love with and for one another. Research shows time and time again, positive social buffers make a significant difference in health and happiness.

Take the story of Sally, for example. Sally was a strong leader and loving mom. She was amazing at her job and a caring parent but had personal relationship struggles. Her marriage was essentially broken. Due to over-giving of herself and poor boundaries, many friendships wound up being energy draining because of how codependent they were. Despite being an incredibly compassionate and independent woman, she was mostly feeling exhausted and resentful; she lived in a constant state of anxiety. Since everything was on her shoulders, she couldn't stop to breathe or slow down for fear a "ball would get dropped," and it'd be all her fault. All she wanted was to feel clear, connected, and at peace inside herself.

Sally had rarely ever invested time into taking care of herself. She started the process of bringing in external support slowly. Self-help books, online groups, and talking to a friend about her own needs were all parts of her gradual process. It took years before she was ready to invest in accountability and support through coaching. Being open to not only allow herself to receive accountability and high level support from someone outside of herself, but actually investing time, money and resources into it – well, that was novel and scary! When you've become accustomed to being taken advantage of by others, it can feel overwhelming to be in a position where you're not just receiving but you're *requesting* the outside accountability and support.

After working together and helping Sally connect with her core values consistently and effectively, all areas of her life began to change. Despite trying to handle everything on her own for so long, she started to delegate more at work and at home. Delegation, when used intentionally, is an effective way of incorporating accountability and support systems within life. She started to speak up and ask for what she needed from her partner rather than give the cold shoulder. This allowed him to learn how to become an external support to her, which he had previously wanted to do but had no idea how. Once Sally opened herself up to the possibility that external support and accountability from others could be helpful rather than harmful, the weight began to lift from her shoulders. Not so suddenly, but still very evidently, she began to realize she didn't have to bear the weight of the world all on her own two shoulders forevermore.

It's important to note, although Sally created a variety of accountability and support systems in her life, she didn't let just anyone into her personal sphere. She didn't go around willy-nilly asking people to hold her accountable for her personal goals or to serve as support systems for everything she wants. She was very deliberate about who she chose to invite into her intimate space. Accountability and support can help in both the work and home settings. However, when it comes to matters close to the heart, getting external support or requesting outward accountability from someone is a gift. Choose your personal accountability and support person(s) with intent. Choose wisely; but when you choose, allow them to support you. Be willing to humbly receive the accountability and support they offer.

If there is too much negativity or harsh criticism from the accountability and support person(s) you choose, it's either not the right fit, not the right time, or the request needs to be communicated differently. If Sally's partner incessantly berated her anytime she asked for help, she'd pull back from asking for certain support because it wouldn't feel safe to do so. Had Sally continued to give her partner the cold shoulder, he would have continued to operate in the dark. It's not that he couldn't be a helpful support; he just didn't know how. If you invite someone in to be a part of your external accountability system in any capacity and there is a pattern of ongoing negativity or hurtfulness, it's not helpful or healthy. This doesn't mean they can never be a healthy accountability or support partner for you, but now may not be the time for them to do so. No matter what, how you choose to communicate your accountability and support needs is up to you.

As Sally grew to feel more deeply supported by both her internal and external accountability systems, her anxiety was reduced. The reduced stress and anxiety gave way to greater creativity and confidence at both work and home. The benefit quickly showed as she began having more quality, fun time with her partner and kids while simultaneously receiving rewards and bonuses at work, the latter of which seemingly came out of nowhere.

The story of Sally is not with regard to one specific person. Unfortunately, Sally's story is a common one and therefore demonstrates the stories of so many women I've worked with and spoken to. Of course, men are no exception to the impact that a lack of proper accountability and support can have on one's entire life experience either. No matter who you are, at one point in time, there will be a need for some form of external accountability and support. This need will ebb and flow because life happens in seasons. Thus, the ebb and flow is both expected and normal.

POINT TO PONDER #26
Accountability Benefits

Accountability and support of all kinds can help you to better manage your time, your commitments, your relationships, your mental health, your physical health, your work-life balance, and so forth. Sally allowed her partner to support her in specific ways, by communicating more clearly about what she needs and why. This helped her feel less anxious and resentful at home. She also increased her use of both accountability and support systems at work by delegating more. This helped her free up time and mental energy which led her to be more focused on and productive with other important tasks.

In what ways may you see benefits, direct or indirect, tangible or intangible, if you introduce or strengthen support and accountability outside of yourself along with the internal checks and balances you've already been setting up for yourself? You do not have to identify exactly how the support or added accountability will need to look right now. Instead, just focus on the potential benefits you may experience if you asked for or allowed support and accountability in a different way than you currently are.

If I allowed myself to receive more or different accountability and support from others, it may benefit me in various ways and in different areas like . . .

My health: *(ex. I may feel less fatigued because I'd over-work myself less.)*

My wealth: *(ex. I may earn more money because I'd free up mental space to get more creative about my work and ways to earn.)*

My intimate relationships: *(ex. I may feel more connected to my partner and have better sex because I won't be so in my head about how annoyed I am about the thing he/she didn't help with.)*

_____

_____

_____

My work: *(ex. Extra accountability would probably help me to finally follow through with presenting this idea I've been putting of proposing at work.)*

_____

_____

_____

My friendships: *(ex. If I had just one person who'd support me and hold me accountable to say no to ___, I'd feel so much less drained and maybe even find a way to walk away from that unhealthy relationship.)*

_____

_____

_____

My mood and overall happiness: *(ex. I'd probably feel much less stressed and be able to have more fun in my day to day.)*

_____

_____

_____

Recite and affirm out loud at least three times today (starting now). Plug a reminder into your phone so you don't forget: "I'm of value and am committed to myself and my health."

SUPPORTS AND ACCOUNTABILITY: INVESTIGATE AND IMPLEMENT.

Okay, so you've explored some of the areas you could use additional or different support and accountability in. You've also explored whether you've allowed yourself to ask for and receive both accountability and support historically, as well as some of the reasons why it may be helpful for you to address any gaps with this at this time. We took time to sort and sift through all of this data so you could have the information you need to make an intentional decision for what will best serve you and your RESET. Now it's time to make some decisions.

What area are you willing to accept or add some external accountability for? What about support additions or changes? Have any ideas surfaced about what this might really look like for you? Remember, everyone's life journey is different, so how you choose to increase accountability or alter support, may look different than how your sibling, parent, best friend or colleague does.

I've shared that, for me, some of the ways I built up outside accountability and support was by investing in therapy, a house cleaning service, and a coaching program. I also practiced opening the lines of communication with my partner more, so I could verbalize what support I needed. I didn't do it all at once. I did them over a period of time that made sense for me, my season of life, and my evolution of self-growth.

The same will be true for you. There are many ways you could build up your external support and accountability, but you can't do them all at once (and even if you could, it's not recommended). Research in human behavior and studies in neuroscience show us that taking small but intentional and consistent steps is much more effective than trying to "fix" or "change" everything all in one heaping jump. In other words, don't try to add in a ton of accountability for every goal you have and then topple on a bunch of random supports you think will make things go faster. That method will not work. Start with one area of challenge, one way to add-in external accountability and one way to allow yourself to ask for or receive support from someone else.

It might feel like I'm harping on this accountability and support topic a bit longer than needed. Perhaps it feels annoying, confusing or maybe even uninteresting to you. Understandable. When I was in my height of "go it alone" mentality, I was highly annoyed by stuff like this too. Hang in there; it *will* make a difference; I assure you. It's helpful to understand what outside accountability may look like for you so you can aptly use and prioritize your support for the highest efficiency. If your health and happiness are struggling, they are of top priority and need to have support and accountability focused upon them ASAP.

Why?

Because your health and happiness are foundational to how the rest of the things in your life get handled; how they get experienced, too. If you're psychologically or spiritually unwell, no matter how hard you try at other things (like relationships or making money), it will not help you feel better, and you'll continue to feel unfulfilled, restless, or just plain *blah*!

POINT TO PONDER #27
My Accountability List

Accountability systems and support people come in all shapes and sizes. They can come in the form of an individual, group, service or even a written scheduler. Typically, the more personal the thing you're seeking support and accountability for, the fewer people there are involved.

So today, dive in and create your very own external support and accountability list! The steps to follow for this exercise are listed below and there's space provided after these steps for you to write your responses.

1. If you have not yet chosen one particular area of your life to home in on for added external accountability and support, do so now.

2. Make a list of potential ways you could introduce or enhance external support and accountability for your chosen area in life. (For example: jogging partner, gratitude text exchange, therapy, coaching, chore chart for kids, enlisting a babysitter, hiring help, attending a support group, etc.)

3. Go back through the list and highlight the ones you believe would have the most impact for you. Which may provide the most relief or help you to experience the feeling of most support at this time?

4. Go back over the list of highlighted ones and rank them in order of which you're most willing to invest your time, money, and efforts.

5. As you move throughout your day and week, other ideas may come to you. Add to the list as needed and repeat the prioritization process.

Space is provided below for you to use as you follow each of these steps.

1. The area of my life I choose to incorporate external accountability and support in is:

2. Ideas about ways to introduce more outward support and accountability are:

_____

_____

_____

_____

_____

_____

_____

_____

_____

_____

_____

_____

_____

_____

_____

_____

_____

_____

_____

_____

3. The ideas I highlighted because they seem like they'd help the most are:

_____

_____

_____

_____

_____

_____

_____

_____

4. I rank my willingness to invest my time, money, and efforts in these external accountability and support options, in this order:

_____

_____

_____

_____

_____

_____

_____

_____

_____

_____

5. Other ideas that have come to mind for me as I pondered about this throughout my week:

_____

_____

_____

_____

_____

_____

_____

_____

After reflecting on all of the information I've gathered here, I've decided:

_____

_____

_____

_____

_____

_____

_____

Recite and affirm out loud at least three times today (starting now). Plug a reminder into your phone so you don't forget: "I'm of value and am committed to myself and my health."

BUT, WHAT IF?!

You've identified which areas you'd like to focus on creating a stronger external accountability system for. You created a list of ways you could introduce or enhance this external support and accountability to help you enjoy your life more. Often, neither of these is easy to do. If you've been real with yourself up until this point, congratulations to you! Most people walk through life without ever having done a fraction of this self-work. By coming this far, you're already more equipped to navigate the stressors of life and to hit your own RESET button than most!

At this point, it's not uncommon to have *"what if"* or *"but"* pop up. Maybe you're unsure any of the support or accountability ideas you've considered will actually work. Maybe you're questioning this whole RESET process because there's some things going on that've brought up frustration for you. Know that any resistance, frustration or doubts are part of the human experience, and one of the most common times for them to strongly pop up is when you're on the precipice of change.

The *"but, what if…"* and *"yeah, but…"* types of thoughts tend to pop up when your old ways of doing and seeing things are being threatened. Questions of doubt that creep in are just your old way feeling the impact of your new way. This is normal. It's a form of resistance that happens when tradition feels threatened by novel methods, which is basically what is happening. Your traditional ways of seeing, doing and believing were challenged in this RESET process, and those that needed updating are being updated. The resistance looks and feels different for each of us, but it's a phenomenon of the change process. Doubt-induced thoughts pop up to keep you in the familiar zone even when it's not really what you want.

I could have easily talked myself out of going to therapy. In fact, I had talked myself out of it in the past. I'd tell myself things like, *I don't have enough time* or *I can't waste my money on that* or, *They won't be able to help me anyway.* Sally could have talked herself out of being more open with her husband. She could have let thoughts like, *He should already know this*, or, *I've already said it a million times*, get in the way of expressing her needs to her partner in a more clear, consistent, and compassionate way. If we had let those thoughts take over and make the decision for us, we'd still feel stuck.

Having thoughts like those is not the real issue. You did not do anything wrong. The real problem that needs to be addressed is how you deal with these kinds of thoughts. If you notice any *"but"* or *"what if"* type of resistance coming up, call them out.

POINT TO PONDER #28
Calling Out the Barriers to Accountability

Call out any thoughts creeping in and trying to prevent you from creating a good external accountability and support set-up for yourself. If left unaddressed, they can and often do steer people away from what they want.

Notice the *"what if"*, *"yeah but"* and other thoughts that are getting in the way of moving forward in this next part of your RESET process. Time and money are often brought up as barriers to fuel these kinds of thoughts.

For example:

Yeah, I want to invest in coaching but it's going to cost too much money.

What if I invest in therapy but I just don't have the time to commit to sessions?

Another common barrier that gets attached to these kinds of thoughts has to do with trust, like *Yeah, I'm willing to invest the money and the time to work with someone who can actually help, but I'm just going to be disappointed. I doubt anyone can actually help me with this.*

Call these kinds of barrier-focused thoughts out and write them down.

Am I experiencing some resistance-based thoughts? What are they?

_____

_____

_____

_____

_____

_____

_____

_____

_____

_____

What do these thoughts seem most worried about? That I won't have enough time to invest in what I know I want to invest in? Money? Trust issues? Some other potential doubt or barrier?

_____

_____

_____

_____

_____

_____

_____

_____

If the worries are mostly around time, what are some ideas I have about how to make more time so I can invest in the accountability or support I think will most help me?

_____

_____

_____

_____

_____

_____

_____

_____

_____

_____

Is there a money barrier? When I think outside of the box, can I find a way to spend less, spend differently, or creatively barter? Am I viewing this as an investment with long-term benefits as a luxury I can't afford, or as an unnecessary expense? Which perspective is most helpful to me right now?

Is there a barrier around trust? How so? Do I trust myself to discern who and what to trust and when to walk away, if need be? How might I address this?

Is there a knowledge or access barrier? Am I just unsure about where to go or how to begin? If I'm unsure where to find the support, could I ask for recommendations, email a professional, or dedicate thirty minutes of my time to doing my own research? Some other thoughts I have about how to navigate this are:

Do the potential benefits of adding on or making changes to my current external accountability and support set-up outweigh the potential risks? Why or why not?

Resistance-based justifications can steer you away from your RESET path and keep you stuck, but only if you buy into them and allow them to be the reasons why you make all of your decisions. Trust your internal guidance to help you discern when, how and with whom you'll make accountability and support adjustments.

Recite and affirm out loud at least three times today (starting now). Plug a reminder into your phone so you don't forget: "I'm of value and am committed to myself and my health."

When I finally said *yes* to invest in therapy, I found myself looking forward to the sessions. I held myself accountable to be real with my therapist. Me showing up in this less guarded way allowed her to be a more effective support to me. She held space for me when I needed to cry, and she held space for me when I just needed to be seen and heard. Undeniably, this helped me feel and practice trusting someone outside of myself and connecting more deeply, which had been a big part of my desired RESET to begin with. My therapist also offered me different perspectives to help hold me accountable for how my decisions may impact those around me. I needed both my internal and external accountability systems to move through this part of my RESET process.

I still remember the one session where I shared a personal story with her about a time I'd felt dismissed and misunderstood during my childhood. She looked directly at me with genuine care in her eyes and said just a few simple words with her nurturing demeanor. She said "That must have been so hurtful. You must have felt so alone."

As simple as those words were, they meant so much to the parts of me that were still in pain and holding on to being that super strong woman as a result of some of those childhood experiences. In those moments, her support gave me an opportunity to feel seen, heard and held with care. Her acknowledgement of my pain, without questioning or doubting it, was powerful. In those moments, I didn't need to be the strong one who hid her emotions. I could cry, and that would be alright. And so, I said: "Yeah, it was", and I cried. I cried a lot. I cried in front of someone, which for me, was not a common experience. But I needed that cry. It helped me release pent up emotions and negativity I needed to let go of.

Conversely, in a separate session, my super independent, armored up part of me was clearly coming up in a scenario I was explaining about a disagreement I'd had with my partner that week. "I guess I'll just have to take care of it all by myself, like always", my guardedness was evident. My therapist held me accountable for noticing how my own stubbornness and challenges were getting in the way and preventing me from seeing a different perspective. During that season of my life, her support and accountability helped me in so many ways.

RECONNECTING TO YOUR STRENGTHS.

You've done a heck of a job discovering what external resources may help you, why, and how. Be gentle but consistent with yourself throughout the process. Enlisting external support and accountability will feel easier for some and much harder for others.

To help you along the way, remember we *all* have internal strengths, resources, and core values that can help us navigate life and enjoy it! However, we can very easily forget about these internal skills and gifts. When we forget about them, we don't use them very wisely. They don't get put to good use, and it winds up hurting us in the long run.

Today, think about what your strengths are. You've been encouraged throughout this program to think of your strengths, and you're being encouraged today to further expand here. As you have been more consciously observant about you and your internal strengths, you'll become more aware of those you may have passed over. Just as you can benefit from allowing others to serve as external support using their strengths, you can use your strengths to support others.

You're using some of your strengths already. Recognize where you're already using your strengths, how they are helpful to you and your life, and which ones you may need to tap into even more.

POINT TO PONDER #29

Strengths + Accountability = Stronger Together

You've already been asked to explore your strengths in this RESET process, so you do know they exist. Today you're reflecting on your strengths again, because it becomes easy to glaze right over them after you've spent some time focusing in on areas of challenge. By revisiting your strengths while you're actively being open to more support and accountability, you create space for both internal and external support to serve you simultaneously.

Explore these prompts and honestly reply:

What strengths do I view myself as possessing?

_____

_____

_____

_____

_____

_____

What area of my life am I feeling strongest in supporting myself with right now?

_____

_____

_____

_____

_____

_____

_____

How so? What evidence do I have to demonstrate this self-support?

Might my strengths be used to serve as a part of someone else's external support or accountability system? Are they already? How so?

Recite and affirm out loud at least three times today (starting now). Plug a reminder into your phone so you don't forget: "I'm of value and am committed to myself and my health."

CHAPTER RECAP

Your internal checks and balances are foundational and absolutely vital to your RESET. External support and accountability enhances the power and effectiveness of your internal support system and can aid it when struggling. There are many ways to introduce or enhance external resources; get creative and choose one or two to get started. As you seek to develop or strengthen your external accountability system, remember resistance is a normal part of growth. When you notice resistance, don't ignore it. Call it out and notice it for what it is. Don't let it stop your progress. If you feel it, it means you're growing (aka RESETTING)!

You have strengths. Use them.

CHAPTER INSIGHTS

The most challenging parts for me in this chapter were:

_____

_____

_____

_____

_____

_____

_____

_____

_____

_____

These were so challenging because:

_____

_____

_____

_____

_____

_____

_____

_____

_____

Am I committed to using my own internal strengths while also enlisting external resources to help myself? Why or why not?

_____

_____

_____

_____

_____

_____

_____

_____

_____

_____

To help myself, I'm choosing to make the following commitments about external accountability and support for me? Because…**Write your commitment down and seal the deal with your signature. This is a commitment between you and you.**

_____

_____

_____

_____

_____

_____

_____

_____

_____

_____

_____

_____

_____

_____

_____

Signed: _____ Date: _____

Recite and affirm out loud at least three times today (starting now). Plug a reminder into your phone so you don't forget: "I'm of value and am committed to myself and my health."

Chapter Seven:

Core Concept Six: The Missing Link

You're more connected to both your inner and outer strengths now that you've taken time to craft an accountability and support set-up to help you inside and out. This is a major step and can't be underestimated. Tapping into our accountability systems is necessary for a high-quality life experience. Our willpower to stick with hard stuff dwindles throughout the day; it's not an unending flow. Therefore, when stress happens and flares up our old habits making them want to kick into gear, it's helpful to already have an accountability system set up so you can tap into it with less effort. This pre-established foundation of support will not just help you stay on track, but when you fall off track, it'll help you get back on more quickly. Yet, I discovered that even these support and accountability systems had their limitations. There was one all-purpose support system that stood above all others, and I could sense the absence of my connection with it.

In this chapter, you'll learn about the unexpected core concept that helped me enhance my RESET process beyond what I'd expected. It's universal, but it's also the key to life satisfaction that's most often misconstrued, misunderstood or just flat out missed in some way. And so, we'll refer to this core concept as the missing link.

Before I continue, let me be clear that although this RESET process is set up as an eight-week journey, my initial RESET was not completed in eight weeks. I learned the process through my own trial and error over the course of several years. I was discovering this process without even realizing what I was doing. Figuring all of this out took me quite some time, but I've now incorporated these RESET steps into my life many times over. Each time I do so, it's this core concept that brings me deeper and surprises me in the most profound of ways everytime! If you take your time with this core concept, I believe it will do the same for you.

During my initial RESET process, taking time to love and reconnect with myself regularly and use my accountability systems had helped me continue to grow into a more enhanced version of myself. Yet, I could still feel something was missing. Things were much better, but I felt like they could be even better. They could go even deeper. It was hard to describe what I felt, but I felt it nonetheless. There was a link missing. It was hard to put my finger on, but I could feel it. Rather, I could feel the absence of my connection to it.

What in the world was it?

IT WAS MY MISSING LINK.

As the daughter of multiple pastors, God, church, and religion were regular parts of my up-bringing. However, while I did have faith, I'd formulated my own ideas about God, church and religion respectively. And my ideas didn't seem to fit with what other people were saying or doing within the church. I felt a sort of internal incongruence and disconnect. I'd see and hear the words "unconditional love" and "forgiveness" be set as moral and religious expectations, but then see actions and hear words of hate and disgust coming from the same place. The disconnect and incongruence I felt was discernible to me. It was something I could see and feel at a young age. Although I didn't have the words for it as a child, I could still feel it. I realized my idea of God was far different from what I was being taught about religion and as a pastor's kid.

I had faith—deep faith. But something about religion didn't sit right with me. Over time, my idea of church and religion had become tainted. I had questions. I had reservations. I had frustrations.

Yet, at a particular time in my RESET journey, I was being brought back to explore my concept of God and the role church played in my life. Rather than through the lens of religion, this exploration steered me toward the power and meaning of connection; deep connection. I'm talking about real, purposeful, intimate connection. There was a yearning for connection and a sense that it could be uniquely satisfied *only* through this missing link. I'm not talking about a frou-frou connection; I'm talking about a distinctive yet ubiquitous connection that connected me to me, while also connecting me to others and to my purpose simultaneously. It sounds abstract, but I felt it so palpably.

Despite the self-growth work I'd done up until that point, I could feel a connection missing—a gap in connection that could be felt, not tangibly measured.

A connection to a higher power.

A connection to something greater than me.

Initially, I did experience some skepticism about making too much meaning out of this path of interest. But eventually the air of mystery and excitement pulled me in. *Where will this take me? What does this mean?* I thought to myself as I ventured this path with pieces of my past church experiences popping up here and there. *I want to know where this is taking me.*

Now, my belief that I'm part of something greater and we are all interconnected in some magnificent way beyond my understanding—well, that has always rang true for me. It still does. But, I had lost sight of what that belief meant for me and my life. Connection with this belief was still there, but it had become blunted over the years, and I wasn't exactly sure what to do with or about it.

It turned out; this all had to do with my missing link! Connecting with a greater power, a source bigger than me, *that* was the deeper connection I was feeling and yearning for. Through a series of unspoken, overt and magical-like experiences, I discovered that the absence of connection I was feeling was me having closed the valve on the pipe to my spiritual, not religious, connection.

The spiritual piece of this whole thing called life had fallen to the wayside because it had gotten so muddled down in mainstream culture that I didn't connect with it there. My views about God had been so different from what I'd seen or heard before, so I'd been unsure how to even begin trying to explain it to myself, let alone explain it to others.

Most people have their own set of ideas and ideals when it comes to things like spirituality or religion. If it seems yours are bumping up against anything I've shared so far, I'm going to challenge you via extension of an invitation. I invite you to set the resistance aside as best you can for these next few moments. I'm not asking you to abandon your ideals, but I *am* asking you not to use them as a barrier to your heart for the time being. I'm asking you to open your mind and heart to the message I share here so you can see what feels true at the core of who you are as you consider these words. I ask that you only seek to integrate into your heart, mind, and life, what feels good and true to you.

Regardless of what you call the higher power you believe in, and regardless of whether you actually believe there is a higher power or not, there are some things we do now know. We know we are all made up, at the minute level, of atoms and energy. Energy is always flowing; it interacts and responds to infinite amount of energy that surrounds it. Science has demonstrated this many times. At the very least, what this tells us is that even though we can't see the stuff we're made of, we are all indeed made up of the same stuff.

If we are all made up of the same stuff, then we must all come from the same source. If we all come from the same source, we must all be connected, in some deeply complex and meaningful way, beyond what our eyes can see. To take it a step further, if we are all made up from the same stuff (energy) and we know that stuff is constantly flowing and interacting, then we all must be able to energetically impact one another, someway and somehow. This is a sensible conclusion, is it not? Whether you call the source from which we come God, the Universe, Allah, the Divine, the Big Bang or something else, the basic premise that we are all interconnected beyond what our eyes can physically see, still stands.

Science also shows us that our bodies are constantly striving for a state of equilibrium or balance. Our body seeks to heal when it's hurt. It seeks to protect when under threat. Those white blood cells seek to absorb the bacteria that make us sick. Our body's natural state is one of balance; that is, a state of wellness or homeostasis.

With this information, we can discern at least three key takeaways:

- We are all created from the same source.

- We are all connected to one another.

- We all want to feel balanced; wellness is the base state we constantly seek to experience.

Even if you don't believe in a higher power, or if your idea of a higher power differs from mine, what I've discovered matters the most about the missing link has nothing to do with what you call it. What matters the most is you know and believe that we are all connected to one another, to our world, and to a larger main source in some significant and meaningful way. This intangible interconnectedness is so significant, in fact, that disconnection from it is unavoidably and deeply felt. It causes the missing link experience.

A lack of connection to the source from whence our atomic energies came, and a lack of awareness about our interconnectedness, leaves us feeling this hard-to-explain, intangible, internal sense that there's something missing.

The missing link is not about religion. Faith and connection to a higher power are not about religion. Unfortunately, religious messages have served as sources of internal shame for many people I speak to and work with. Messages of condemnation about how they "should be" and "shouldn't be" lead them to feel bad about themselves rather than loved, worthy, or empowered. This kind of messaging does not make way for the balance we all innately desire down to our most minute level. No, it does quite the opposite. Instead, it exacerbates or creates mental health, communication, and relationship issues. While some may indeed find a connection to their missing link through religion, this core concept is not about religion; it's about connection.

"Missing link" doesn't mean there's no link between you and your higher power. It means that you've not been plugging into or staying connected with your link in a deliberate and nurturing way. The link between you and your higher power never actually goes away; it's impossible, as it's the source of life. However, we can forget it's there; we can try to deny it; we can attempt to take control of our own lives and not turn towards it. When we don't intentionally take time strengthening this link of connection, it feels like it goes missing because we aren't utilizing it enough or at least not effectively.

POINT TO PONDER #30

Belief Exploration: The Missing Link

Reflecting on what you've read about the missing link so far, get curious about your own reactions to and beliefs about it.

Honestly respond to these prompts with an open heart and open mind.

What do I believe? Do I believe there is some kind of greater power/force/energy/ source than myself?

Why do I or don't I believe this?

_____

_____

_____

_____

_____

_____

_____

_____

_____

_____

Is this a new way or old way of me looking at things? How long have I thought this way and how open am I to expanding my beliefs on this?

_____

_____

_____

_____

_____

_____

_____

What might my beliefs about this mean for me, my life, or my connection with others? Does it have any impact at all? Do I want it to have an impact? Why or why not?

Recite and affirm out loud at least three times today (starting now). Plug a reminder into your phone so you don't forget: "I have purpose. My life is meaningful."

Different people use different terminology to describe their higher power. For ease of communication, the term "the missing link" will be used interchangeably to reference all terminology described under the "higher power" umbrella of terms, such as God and the Universe.

FAITH. TRUST. CONNECTION.

Simply put, closing the gap in connection between you and your missing link requires faith, trust, and belief in something greater than yourself. What exactly you call that may be different than what others call it. Some people call it God; others call it Source, the Universe, a greater energy or power, Creator, etc. Personally, I have shifted in the names I've used over the course of my life. God. Creator. Source. Since I stay open to learn and evolve, it's possible I may shift what label I use again at some point.

It's not for me to tell you what name to use or even what to believe. What I'm here to share with you is about the power and purpose that's only available through this more ethereal level of connection. A deeper sense of connection to something greater than you which also connects you with the world and others around you – it creates opportunity for a more meaningful life and profound clarity on how worthy and purposeful your existence truly is intended to be.

The more I sought to close the gap between myself and my missing link, the more realizations I had. One such realization was if I was created from it then the power of it must also be part of me. If the power of this energy source was part of me, then it was within me somehow. Always. If I had that power within me, there must be a way for me to tap into it. Surely, if I can tap into the kind of power that creates life, worlds and the universe, then I couldn't be that powerless. I couldn't just be a victim of circumstance. I couldn't just be a servant to crappy conditions beyond my control. I realized, if that power was part of me, I must be able to use it to help in my life as well as others. If I tapped into it, I'd be able to experience a deeper sense of purpose and focus for all parts of my life.

In retrospect, there have indeed been times in my life when things felt hard and completely out of control—unbearable even. Yet, something I hadn't planned and couldn't explain had happened and wound-up changing things in a weird but ultimately supportive way. Like, when I was in college and questioned whether I should still be alive or not. I was hospitalized, and some random person gave my mother a handmade flag with a heart on it. Even though that woman didn't know me and didn't know I was in the hospital, she told my mom she made that special flag of hope for me, her daughter. My mom gave it to me when I was released from the hospital. I still don't know who made it, yet it was so meaningful and timely. I'd asked for a sign that I still had purpose here on earth, and that unexpected, hand sewn flag was one way that sign was delivered.

A few years later, I got into a car accident during a horrible icy snowstorm. My daughter and I had been waiting in the car for a while for the police to come. Out of nowhere, and for what seemed like no reason, I got the urge to get my daughter and myself out of the car and wait on the side of the road. The decision didn't make sense at first. My daughter was young, and it was cold and snowy outside. But I got us out anyway. The moment I did, another car came sliding in and slammed into the back of my car. Had we been inside of it, we would have certainly been significantly injured. The car was totaled. It was terrifying, but we were safe. We had gotten out of the car just in time.

The more I got curious about my missing link, what it was, and what it meant for me and my life, the more I felt mysteriously supported. After feeling alone, unsupported, and misunderstood for most of my life, the concept of a link between me, everyone else, and the source that creates worlds, was oddly comforting. It wasn't that I'd ever stopped believing in my God. I had maintained my faith over the years. It was just that my understanding of who and what God as the universal source of energy meant for me, was different than it once was. Since my understanding had changed, so too did my relationship with it. Consciously shifting my perspective about how this source, me and we are all connected, reignited my belief in myself and my worth. It helped me practice more acceptance, compassion, and love towards myself in a deeper way than I'd ever felt before.

I experienced a deeper knowing; I had a kind of inner guidance and support system extending beyond what my rational or logical mind could think up. My missing link was a deeper layer than the internal accountability system I'd been working on. Connecting with my missing link in a different way than I had before, changed my inside world in a magnificent way. It helped me develop a renewed, incredibly profound sense that no matter the circumstance, I had the support of my source there at the ready. This power source was mysteriously yet reliably available to help me navigate whatever terrain I may intentionally or unintentionally wander into.

The power surge I felt as I reconnected with my missing link wasn't about control; it wasn't like I felt I could use the power to manipulate everything or change everyone. It wasn't as if I suddenly thought I could become omnipotent myself or solve all of the world's problems. No, this power that comes from connecting with the missing link isn't about righteousness or dominance; in many ways it's the opposite. For me, it was a deeper level of knowing and trusting that I had an invisible support system available to me; always and forever. A support system that cared about my wellness and loved me unconditionally, no matter what. I didn't have to earn it. I didn't have to prove anything to it. It was there, it wanted to support me, and I was inherently deserving of it.

It was life-changing enough for me to know I wasn't as alone as I'd felt for most of my life because of this renewed connection to my missing link. But, the impact of this renewed connection was magnified by a deeper knowing that this power extends beyond even that. There was a knowing that, because I'm of the source (God, the Universe, whatever you choose to call that great energy), I must be innately capable, worthy, strong, and with purpose. How could I be created by such a universally impactful power source and not be with power or purpose myself?

Understanding connection in this way reminds us that each of us is connected to everyone else because everyone else has come from this same source. They are worthy, so are you and so am I. They want to live, love and feel well; so do you and so do I. Therefore, how I treat myself *and* how I treat others *both* matter. How you treat yourself and how you treat others, both matter. It can't be just one nor can it be just the other. How we treat ourselves and how we treat others matters because we are all connected, our stuff can impact other people's stuff, and all of our lives have purpose.

It's hard to describe what the rekindled connection with my missing link meant for me; yet I think it's supposed to be that way. Some experiences are beyond mere words. They are just felt. Your experiences will be yours. Allow yourself to feel them.

One clear way these realizations affected my life was in how I updated my understanding of my core values. The inner shift in perspective I experienced through this process helped me conceptualize the meaning of my core values in an even deeper way. As a result, I more effectively applied my core values as I managed various life situations. My core values of compassion and forgiveness needed to be applied to me as well as to others. Your core values need to be applied in your connection with yourself, as well as with others. The missing link is the link that connects us all. When we are truly tapping into it, we are all able to share and experience values like compassion and forgiveness in profound and sincere ways.

POINT TO PONDER #31

The Missing Link Enhances Core Values

Applying your understanding and beliefs of what the missing link means for you and your life can help you optimize how you use your core values. Consider how you may bring the missing link and your core values together by reading, reflecting, and writing your response to the questions below.

Have I been treating myself as if I'm worthy, invaluable, and with purpose? Or have I been judging myself too harshly, without compassion and without forgiveness?

Have I been treating others as if they are worthy, valuable, and with purpose? Or have I been judging others too harshly, without compassion and without forgiveness?

Have I been applying my core values within my relationship with myself as a worthy individual, and have I been doing the same with others? How so?

_____

_____

_____

_____

_____

_____

_____

_____

_____

_____

_____

_____

_____

_____

_____

_____

_____

_____

Recite and affirm out loud at least three times today (starting now). Plug a reminder into your phone so you don't forget: "I have purpose. My life is meaningful."

Recognizing there was a gap in connection between me and my higher power served as a reminder that we're all indeed connected to one another, and we all have purpose. I'm not an accident, and neither are you. Therefore, I was going to make sure I lived the kind of life I wanted to live, being the kind of person I wanted to be. I'd take the time to connect with me because it allowed me to connect with the power within me as well as those around me.

CONNECTING WITH YOUR MISSING LINK.

How can we connect with this missing link if it's invisible?

That's a good question. When we can't actually see, hear, physically touch, or taste something, it's easy to be skeptical about its existence. How can you connect with something you can't see, touch, taste, or hear? Even if you believe in it already, how can you deliberately plug into it and optimally utilize its power for inspiration and support?

You have to slow down, grow quiet, and feel. That's why various forms of mindfulness and meditation are such effective forms of connecting to your missing link. A *felt sense* is one that we are often taught to ignore in some way, but it's not supposed to be avoided. Your felt sense is your first to develop as a human, and it's also the key to connecting with your missing link.

Meditation is a powerful tool to connect inwardly and with your missing link. Meditation is meant to be a safe space where judgment is released, both of yourself and others. Meditation is not about completely controlling all your thoughts like many people tend to believe. Instead of controlling your thoughts, meditation is about accepting them. It calls you to practice letting your thoughts be what they are without exerting your energy to either feed into nor fight against them. If you want to intentionally connect with your missing link, you can do so by releasing your focus on controlling everything, including your own thoughts. Meditation is the practice of creating the space for this to happen.

Part of what makes meditation so powerful is you're deliberately choosing to slow down and release the need for control and judgment. This disconnection from outward chaos allows you to meaningfully connect with inward peace, which is where communication with your missing link can most easily transpire.

The resulting space of acceptance created when you take time to practice meditation or mindfulness, means you no longer have to mentally beat up on yourself nor prove something to yourself or anyone else. Since your missing link won't beat up on you either, the pressure is down. When pressure is down, so are the internal defenses, and in this state connection can prosper. Introducing appreciation and compassion to your practice will amplify your experience. When practiced together, each of these components helps to create a fertile mental and emotional safe haven for you, right there within you. Your missing link is always available for you, if you simply choose to intentionally settle in and deliberately connect.

Prayer can be a form of meditation. Sometimes people use prayer to complain about what's not going well, to make demands, or to ask for things to go "right" or to go "my way." This form of prayer isn't meditative, and it's often not constructive either. Those kinds of prayers are more about trying to grasp for control and less about letting go of it. Remember, the missing link is about support, balance, love, faith, trust and connection. If you're focused on fear, vengeance or control, you're going to have a harder time connecting with your missing link.

One of the reasons connecting in a more intimate, intentional way is so powerful is because we have all become so accustomed to living busy lives. We drive ourselves to sickness as we try to control who and what we can't control. We forget to slow down, to have faith, and to enjoy the present moment. Meditation reminds us of how important this is, and when we do it, we are better able to connect with ourselves. This deeper connection with self allows us to better connect with this universal energy— the missing link.

POINT TO PONDER #32
Ingredients to Connect with My Missing Link

When practiced together, acceptance, presence, appreciation, and compassion foster wellness. These ingredients help you connect with your missing link. In order to practice these components in your daily life, there has to be a willingness to let go of some control over certain things beyond your control. Today, check in with yourself to see if you're using the ingredients needed for intentional connection with the missing link that lives inside of you.

Take your time as you read, reflect and respond to these prompts.

Am I taking time to slow down, have faith, and enjoy the present moment? If not, how can I do more of this? What might it look like for me? What might it require of me?

What's my stance on acceptance? Do I have any resistance about it? Am I working hard to control and therefore not to accept certain things? Am I open to acceptance that there are certain things I can't control? Am I okay with this?

Am I practicing compassion towards myself and others? Why or why not? What makes it hard? What could make it less challenging?

How do I talk or engage with my missing link? Am I mostly just trying to get what I want, express my woes, or avoid what I don't want? Or am I more focused on appreciation and guidance on how I can be more of who I desire to be as a more connected, intentional, and purposeful human being?

_____

_____

_____

_____

_____

_____

_____

_____

_____

_____

_____

_____

_____

_____

_____

_____

Recite and affirm out loud at least three times today (starting now). Plug a reminder into your phone so you don't forget: "I have purpose. My life is meaningful."

CONTROLLED AND SUPPORTED ARE NOT THE SAME.

If this powerful missing link is all about support, balance, and love, and we are all connected through it, then why do bad things happen? This is an understandable and, I believe, age-old question. It's one I have grappled with before too.

When I felt most out of control in my life, I sometimes wondered why things were happening to me. As I grew older and helped individuals and families who'd gone through unthinkable traumas, I'd wondered how something so horrible could happen to them.

I'd been hurt.

I'd seen so many people get hurt.

Time and time again I witnessed that hurt people, hurt people, or they hurt themselves. When people are hurting inside, the hurt shows up on the outside, too; we want something or someone to blame. There needs to be some kind of explanation for all of this, doesn't there? There needs to be some kind of justice served or some kind of fair fix, right?

Although the latter is how our society tends to try to format our systems, this is not really how I've seen the missing link function. Since the missing link is a force of creation, wellness and love, it does not aim to control any of us. This is because the basis of creation, wellness and love is freedom. Inherent in freedom is free-will, which is best used in conjunction with good-will. When good-will is not included in the use of free-will, pain and suffering tend to ensure. God, the creative energy source of the universe, aims to support and guide us toward a path that creates more love and wellness. But the path is not without resistance because it is our free human will that's often grabbed the steering wheel and taken over to gain control of things and make decisions in our lives.

When a hurt human tries to take matters into their own hands, a chain of pain eventually follows. We have a painful experience and then take action against someone from that place of pain. The person we impact feels hurt then goes on to impact another, and so on and so forth. Of course, the path of life is never as clear cut as that, but the truth can't be denied that we all experience and react to pain. We often don't know someone is in pain when they've wronged or hurt us, we just know the hurt we feel, or even the hurt we witnessed someone else endure. As we take action from these places of pain, we are typically taking action outside of our connection to our missing link. We try to exert power and control without truly being connected to the most powerful part within us. That is, we venture outside of the more immediate path to co-creating love, peace and wellness, and onto a detoured, bumpier path riddled with fear and suffering.

While the missing link will create opportunities for a less bumpy road, it's not going to force you to do anything. That would defy our natural right to free-will. When we make choices apart from the support and guidance of this main source of wellness and love, pain and suffering are inevitable.

What I know to be true is we are free to tap into the love and support the missing link has to offer us, and we are free to not tap into it. Easy or hard, we have the choice; even when we don't feel like we do. As the great Dr. and Reverend Martin Luther King Jr stated, "Returning hate for hate multiplies hate, adding deeper darkness to a night already devoid of stars. Darkness cannot drive out darkness; only light can do that. Hate cannot drive out hate; only love can do that."

When we are hurt and not tapping into that deeper source of love and connection, we don't connect with ourselves or one another in the loving way we were meant to. Our focus is on the fear, pain, or uncertainty of the darkness, and so that influence winds up affecting our decisions. These decisions ultimately impact us and those around us. The resulting domino effect is a chain of pain. The link goes missing from our focus, not because it's no longer there, but because we are looking elsewhere. We are no longer slowing down and turning inward enough to tap into it and feel it. Breaking the chain of pain would mean we ourselves would have to get more deliberate about which side, light or dark, faith or fear, love or lack, we are most influenced by *before* we make our decisions.

When we forget or don't realize we all share a common source of connection through our very essence of existing in a world where everything and everyone is made up of energy and atoms, we are missing connection to *the* link. We are missing an opportunity to connect in a different and more meaningful way. However, no one can stay focused on the light of the missing link or tapped into its energy one hundred percent of the time. Being human means being imperfect. Just bring yourself back to an inner knowing that the energy which created us all is a source of wellness and therefore wants wellness for *all* of us. It *is* on your side; it's on the side of balance and wholeness for all living beings.

When thinking about this topic, I'm often reminded of the scene from the movie, *Evan Almighty*. Early in the movie, the wife prayed for her family to grow closer together. Her husband winds up being labeled as "crazy" when he sacrifices his high-paying political position in order to build an ark because "God told me to." The wife takes the kids and leaves but unknowingly bumps into God on earth, who was disguised as her waiter. She's visibly upset, and he says:

"Let me ask you something. If someone prays for patience, do you think God gives them patience? Or does he give them the opportunity to be patient? If he prayed for courage, does God give him courage, or does he give him opportunities to be courageous? If someone prayed for the family to be closer, do you think God zaps them with warm fuzzy feelings, or does he give them opportunities to love each other?"

The wife, wide-eyed, realized that in the midst of the painful challenge her family was facing, she was being given an opportunity to have her former prayer answered. It wasn't going to be easy or smooth, but it was going to be worth it.

I don't think I came into this world as a blank slate. I think I came into this world wanting to be a unifier—a unifier unlike any other who helps people move from a place of feeling trapped and internally suffering to a place of feeling freer and more connected. All my hardships have turned into opportunities for me to learn how to be a better me and a better guide for helping people navigate life as they bridge their gap from trapped to free, from fear to faith, from unsatisfied to fulfilled.

We all get to craft our own lives. Our lives are not being controlled by the missing link. It's not there to punish others nor does it exist to punish you. This missing link is one of support. It's fueled by love, so that's all it will offer. It will guide you towards life experiences that'll provide opportunities to help you become more of who you are and to live more of the life you want to live. The question is, are you paying attention? Are you turned towards the light? Are you taking the time to slow down and tap into it?

POINT TO PONDER #33
What's Influencing My Decisions?

It's human nature to react and defend when we witness, experience or want to avoid hurt, betrayal, or unfair treatment. We all do this. It's challenging to begin to acknowledge when this is happening, but it's an important part of self-growth, and therefore is of significance to your RESET. It can be difficult to think about things in the way these questions are challenging you to consider. Simply allow yourself to notice your reactions, and then openly and honestly respond to the questions below.

Do I more often make decisions by reacting from a place of hurt, anger or distress or by responding from a place of connection, calm, clarity and wellbeing?

What kind of potential hurt, betrayal or unfairness might I be wanting to avoid or prevent? Do I believe connecting with my missing link could ease any challenges I'm having with this?

Do I have any doubts about my missing link? Any fears? Anger? Resentment? Confusion?

_____

_____

_____

_____

_____

_____

_____

_____

_____

_____

_____

_____

_____

_____

_____

Choose to spend a few moments intentionally connecting with your missing link, using whatever means work best for you. Perhaps you'll give meditation or mindfulness a try. If you have a meditation or mindfulness practice already, I encourage you to introduce variety by trying a different form of meditation or mindfulness today.

Recite and affirm out loud at least three times today (starting now). Plug a reminder into your phone so you don't forget: "I have purpose. My life is meaningful."

A DIFFERENT KIND OF CONNECTION.

When we don't feel connected, we don't feel good.

The innate need for connection is at the very basis of our human nature. When we don't feel meaningfully connected, we look for ways to feel it (whether those ways are healthy or not). As convenience, immediacy and high levels of productivity have increasingly taken precedence in our culture, the unfortunate result has been that many ways of connecting are superficial.

Superficial connections don't feel fulfilling. Like, when I was in my prime people-pleasing mode. I worked hard to avoid confrontation or to diffuse any conflict because I didn't want to feel misunderstood or rejected. I'd worry, *I hope they didn't misunderstand me. I don't want to seem difficult. Should I even say anything? Do they really even care what I have to say? They're probably thinking something bad about me. Ugh, let me try again.* And then I'd try to do or say something to make them view me in a different way, even though I really had no idea how they did or did not actually view me in the first place.

The only reason I, or any of us, try to avoid feeling misunderstood or rejected is because we actually want to feel the opposite, which is accepted and connected. People-pleasing serves as a means of trying to be accepted, which really comes from a need to feel connected. The trouble with using people-pleasing as a means of meaningful connection, is that it doesn't work. No one can please everyone, and in trying to please everyone the pleaser winds up sacrificing themselves. People pleasing doesn't allow each person to be their imperfect selves. The resulting connection is conditional, superficial, artificial or flimsy.

If you look back to the fears you explored in Chapter Three, you'll likely find there is a deep desire for connection underlying many of them. If you haven't yet discovered this, the prerequisite is getting courageous enough to dig deeper to unveil it.

POINT TO PONDER #34
Connection Over Impression

All too often we humans, especially my fellow leaders and achievers, can get sucked into acting a certain way in order to make an impression. We convince ourselves (or let others convince us) that first impressions can make or break our current and future chances with those we interact with. At surface level this isn't inherently an issue, but if impressing someone takes precedence over meaningfully connecting with them, then the interaction isn't authentic. The foundation laid is laden with false niceties and unnecessary pressures to act a certain way from thenceforth. The kind of foundation this creates isn't ideal for living a life that feels more free and fulfilled, is it?

In order for these next sections to really hit home for you, you'll need to be willing to embrace meaningful connection as a basic human need. Connection as a basic human need is not a new concept. Abraham Maslow created a hierarchy of needs back in 1954, which demonstrated the needs of love, safety, and belonging as foundational for happiness and healthy human development. Although his original presentation has evolved over the years, the foundational points remain largely unchanged and are widely accepted.

In the space below, I invite you to explore your thoughts around meaningful connection, impressions, and all that comes along with each of them.

What does meaningful connection mean to me? Do I cherish it? Do I desire it? Do I view it as a basic human need?

What would life be like if it was devoid of meaningful connections? Would impressions be sufficient? Why or why not?

Have I experienced meaningful connections with anyone in my life? Who? How so? What makes it meaningful?

When I don't feel meaningfully connected, what do I do? How do I handle it? Do I compensate in some way?

_____

_____

_____

_____

_____

_____

_____

_____

_____

_____

When people I care about don't feel meaningfully connected to me, how do they behave? How might they feel? Why might they feel that way?

_____

_____

_____

_____

_____

_____

_____

_____

_____

_____

Other reflections:

_____

_____

_____

_____

_____

_____

_____

_____

_____

_____

Recite and affirm out loud at least three times today (starting now). Plug a reminder into your phone so you don't forget: "I have purpose. My life is meaningful."

Strengthening connection with the missing link helps us to more meaningfully connect with both ourselves and others. It truly does help to satisfy the need for connection in a way that no one and nothing else can. However, effectively connecting with the missing link generally requires intentionally taking time to connect in a totally different way than how we are taught to by society. Superficial, conditional, or flimsy connection doesn't cut it. You have to be willing to get vulnerable and fully expose yourself when you seek to connect with your missing link.

Vulnerably exposing ourselves calls for *not* needing to be right and *not* trying to be perfect. Good old fashioned people pleasing, self-sacrifice, over-accomplished, and things of the like, won't work when it comes to connecting with the missing link that resides within us. Exposing myself, my fears and my imperfections was challenging for me, even within a private setting between me and my missing link. I'd sometimes judge myself for my own thoughts or feelings. I'd set the standards for myself high and I expected myself to meet those standards. Setting high standards for myself could sometimes leave room for me to get down pretty hard on myself. For me to let my guard down and open myself up more with my own missing link, I had to practice shifting my internal dialogue. I needed to even more deliberately practice connecting with *myself* in a less judgmental way. One at a time, I introduced an attitude of more compassion, gratitude, and acceptance toward myself as I slowed down and turned inward.

I don't quite remember what I said to myself verbatim, but it may have sounded something like, *Hey, it's me. I'm proud of you today. I'm not sure what's next, but I'm learning to trust that things are working out. I know we've got this, even when it's hard, and I feel upset. Thanks for being there.*

As I developed a new way of connecting through myself to my missing link, I felt internal peace and ease more often. Instead of trying to figure everything out and force an outcome through intense effort and control, bit by bit, I started intentionally surrendering some control. I practiced having more faith and trust in this invisible power, which I could feel was part of me (some call this the Holy Spirit, soul, chi, spirit, higher self, or some other term along these same lines).

Ironic how we need to surrender control to tap into more power, isn't it? This whole surrender and vulnerability business took me quite some time to understand. You don't have to do it all at once; you can take your time. But it's hard to connect meaningfully when your guard is up; it's like putting a shield between you and your link. If you're unsure about it like I was, that's fair. That's just where you're at along your journey currently. Your journey will carry on, and you will continue to learn and grow.

There was a particularly vivid moment in my life where the experience of surrendering vulnerably in connection with my missing link led me to feel so intensely tapped into its power. I was practicing meditation years ago and my body progressively got warm and tingly. Seemingly out of nowhere, a statement dropped into my awareness that left me both awestruck and comforted all at once. It's a statement that has stuck with me ever since. It was so calming and so grounding. I never heard it anywhere else. I discerned the words only because I chose to slow down, turn inward, and connect with my link. In those moments, I was open and vulnerable; my link was no longer missing.

The statement I heard was: *It's not about me; I surrender. Although I am supported in this venture, it's not about me; I surrender.* Repeating this statement during challenging times has been the exact thing I've needed to help me reset and refocus many times over. I never would have received those wise words if I hadn't reestablished a deeper and different connection with my missing link. I trust these words may even serve you along your journey in some meaningful way as well.

POINT TO PONDER #35
Surrender and Silence

Surrendering with vulnerability is a hard concept to buy into when you're used to taking action, trying to control things, or always busy seeking a way to "fix", "figure out" or resolve things. Surrendering is a practice of letting go of control; it's not about giving up on your desires or what matters to you. Vulnerability is a willingness to expose yourself, imperfections, and all. Slowing down enough so there can be silence, will allow you to practice more surrender and vulnerability as you connect with your missing link.

Take ten minutes longer than you normally would to simply sit in silence and connect with your link, so it's *not* feeling like it's missing. If you're not sure what that means for you, choose to connect with a memory, dream, or thought that feels like love, support, acceptance, compassion, or gratitude. Surrender to the silence and focus on feeling the goodness of this connection.

After you've taken at least ten minutes to surrender to the silence, write down anything that sticks out to you. Maybe there was a feeling, a thought, or a strong sensation. There's no right or wrong here; just write out your observations without judgment.

_____

_____

_____

_____

_____

_____

_____

_____

_____

Recite and affirm out loud at least three times today (starting now). Plug a reminder into your phone so you don't forget: "I have purpose. My life is meaningful."

In our yearning for connection, we seek and reach for various methods on how to go about getting that need met. Both meaningful human connection and intentional spiritual connection is necessary for a deeper sense of freedom and fulfillment in life. Allow yourself to connect with and lean into whatever your experience with your link is supposed to be for you. Continue to explore your own thoughts and feelings about what "meaningful connection" is and what it looks like for you. If you're into the hard sciences, you can read up on the studies in physics which explore how we're all made up of atoms, originating from ever-flowing energy and emitting and receiving electronic vibrations constantly. Even if the missing link core concept seems "woo-woo" or "too spiritual" for you, the truth of the matter is no matter how you look at it, science, psychology, or spirituality, *we are all connected.*

Everyone will be in a different place when it comes to the relationship with themselves and their missing link. Remember, your RESET journey is your own, and so your experience with your link and how it shows up in your life is always unique to you. It's supposed to be.

Also remember this: there's about a 1 in 400 trillion chance of *you* being born as you. You're not here by accident. Something bigger than you has your back.

POINT TO PONDER #36
Set The Missing Link Alarm

Although connecting to your link may feel like it goes missing from time to time, your lack of connecting to it does not need to stay missing indefinitely. Changing status with your link calls for intentionally taking the time to connect differently, both inwardly (with ourselves) and outwardly (with others and the world around us). You may be called to connect with your link in a way that's contrary to how you've previously been expected or taught throughout your life. Be open to this. To have a different experience than you've had before, you'll either have to try something different or come to the table with a different attitude.

If parts of this exercise seem strange or off-putting for you, it's probably because it's different from what you're used to. That's fine. Keep an open mind and explore where this exercise takes you. If this exercise seems easy because it's a common practice for you, I encourage you to get creative and add another element to deepen your experience.

Practice intentionally turning inward with an attitude of compassion, gratitude, acceptance, and faith. Follow the steps below to guide you:

1. Choose one of the following experiences to get more intentional about: compassion, gratitude, acceptance, faith, love.

2. Every hour, for eight consecutive hours today, take twenty seconds to close your eyes, turn inward, and focus on allowing yourself to connect with the experience you chose. To help remind yourself, you can simply put a reminder on your phone to go off every hour for the next eight hours.

3. When the reminder goes off, think about the experience you chose. Allow yourself to feel it in the moment or reflect on times when you have recently felt it. Taking just twenty to thirty seconds to do this with focused mindfulness is enough. Then go on about your day.

4. At the end of the day, write down what this experience was like for you in the space provided below. If you want to go a step further, write down your observations immediately after each pause, or extend this practice to more than one day.

Recite and affirm out loud at least three times today (starting now). Plug a reminder into your phone so you don't forget: "I have purpose. My life is meaningful."

CHAPTER RECAP

The missing link is available for connection within all of us, it's what connects us all to one another. When we don't value the wellness of ourselves or others, we are choosing not to tap into that connection and the connection to our link feels like it goes missing. Simply put, we are all connected. We all have access to connect with the source that's bigger than, yet within all of us. Therefore, we all have purpose and can live meaningful lives.

You can choose to shift your missing link to a connected link and use it to enhance your life and relationships. You can also choose not to do that. There is no viable substitution for the missing link. The choice is yours. For many, it takes time and intention to learn how to meaningfully connect and tap into the power of the source from which you came. While you can demonstrate the power of the missing link for others, you can't choose it for anyone else. You can't force anyone else to connect with their missing link. You can only choose this for yourself. You can choose this moment by moment.

Practicing compassion, acceptance, love, and gratitude is a sure-fire way to get plugged into your link so you don't feel like that connection is missing. In turn, as you feel more connected to your link from within yourself, you'll be better able to share and experience more compassion, acceptance, love, and appreciation outwardly.

Find a way to connect with a faith that reminds you that you have purpose, because you most certainly do. You're no accident. Your existence is with purpose. Remember, there's about a 1 in 400 trillion chance of *you* being born. Something bigger than you has your back.

Reconnecting with my higher power reminded me that just as much as it lives around me, it resides within me. Always. This understanding bolstered my belief in how powerful I am and can be for both myself and others.

What did you realize? What do you believe?

CHAPTER INSIGHTS

Take time to contemplate and reflect upon the below questions. Write down honest, open, and reflective responses in the space provided.

Does who I aspire to be align with the values of a power that honors and respects all forms of life, love, and nature? Does the life I desire to RESET to, align with this as well?

What does this mean to me? For me? Do I believe it means something about me?

What's at least one thing I'd be willing to begin, to do more of, or to do differently, to help me connect with my missing link even more?

_____

_____

_____

_____

_____

_____

_____

_____

Am I willing to commit to practicing more compassion, gratitude, and acceptance in day-to-day interactions with myself and others, to honor the deeper connections and purpose we all have?

_____

_____

_____

_____

_____

_____

_____

_____

Recite and affirm out loud at least three times today (starting now). Plug a reminder into your phone so you don't forget: "I have purpose. My life is meaningful."

Chapter Eight:

Core Concept Seven: Cultivating Joy

Joy is beyond mere happiness. It's a deeply felt sense of inward pleasure, freedom, and invigoration all wrapped up into one. In this chapter, we focus on cultivating joy!

Before we dive in, let's quickly see what your initial thoughts on joy are. What first comes to mind when you think of joy? What is your immediate reaction to the thought of cultivating joy? Don't overthink it, just notice it and write it down. Is your immediate reaction a sense of disconnect, yearning, reminiscing, scoffing, ecstasy, belief, disbelief, excitement, something else?

Most people don't understand that there is a major (and mandatory) connection between feeling deep, genuine joy and having real love toward themselves. These seem like two separate topics—joy and self-love. However, joy feels either superficial, just out of grasp, or too far from reach when someone doesn't love themselves or own their value as an individual. To experience joy in its purest form, a foundation of unconditional self-love is important. A belief that you're worthy of experiencing joy allows you to experience joy more deeply.

Unconditional love is the basis for joy because it gives you permission to feel, to mess up, to forgive, to have boundaries, to rest, and to live and let live. Essentially, unconditional self-love gives you permission to say, *Hey, I accept that I'm an imperfect human who is always developing, and yet I'm still worthy of love right here, right now!* Unconditional self-love is experienced in moments rather than achieved or completed for a lifetime.

Joy can't be given by someone else; it's internally cultivated. When you're truly feeling joy, you're tapped into your missing link. This is different from feeling happy because something good has been given to you or happened to you. While joy and happiness are both desirable, they are not the same. One can feel happy about many things. Happiness is typically dependent upon external circumstances. Examples might be, "I felt happy when my partner got me that item I'd been wanting for so many years" or "I felt happy when I got that pay raise" or "I'd feel happy if my kids would stop bickering with one another and actually get along!"

If something good happens in your life, you may momentarily feel happy. Joy, however, can endure even when external situations get hard; it need not be contingent upon circumstances. The experience of joy connects you with a sense of purpose and meaning. It's an internal experience you can cultivate now, whether a specific situation is or isn't occurring at the moment. Joy may be felt during times of free-flowing creativity or non-pressured self-expression, like dancing, drawing, singing or crafting. It can also be cultivated through mindful mental appreciation of what you find fun or purpose in.

As an example, I may feel happy when my kids help me around the house. The external condition of them helping is what I'm focused on in this case, and so I feel happy because of that. However, even when I'm not with my children, I can mindfully appreciate motherhood. Regardless of where I'm at, I could choose to bask in my love of them and all that I imagine for them. In this case, although nothing has changed contextually, and no one has done anything to me or for me, I feel joyful.

Happiness and joy both feel good, and both are good. We all want to experience happiness and joy in our lives. While we won't dive too much deeper into the difference between happiness and joy for this RESET process, knowing that joy can be cultivated even when life gets hard or doesn't go as planned, is a game-changer.

As wonderful as joy feels, no one can stay in joy forever. Feeling joy 100% of the time isn't possible, but everyone can learn to tap into it more and more. In fact, part of what makes experiencing joy so amazing is that it doesn't last forever. As a result of its impermanence, joyful moments are all the more special, powerful, and deeply felt.

Although we all have the ability to cultivate joy, we don't all do so in the same way. Learning how to welcome more joy into your life is a process. It's an experiential process just like the rest of your RESET has been. I will share some methods with you which outline how to begin and continue this process, but it's up to you to allow yourself to really *feel* the process. Allowing yourself to experience this process *is* within your power.

POINT TO PONDER #37
Joy

When I think of joy now, what comes to my mind?

_____

_____

_____

_____

_____

_____

_____

_____

_____

_____

_____

_____

_____

Do I feel worthy of experiencing joy? Does it feel okay for me to have joyful experiences? Why or why not?

_____

_____

_____

_____

_____

Recite and affirm out loud at least three times today (starting now). Plug a reminder into your phone so you don't forget: "I love welcoming joy into my life. The more joy I have, the more joy I can share!"

Even though I wanted to experience more joy in my life, I had this hidden fear that experiencing too much of it would somehow make me less productive. Joy seemed like something fun and carefree. It seemed like something I could only have *after* I had accomplished my long to-do list and lofty goals. Joy seemed more like a blissful reward I needed to work hard to earn but had no time in the present to enjoy. It seemed almost luxurious, like it was something I couldn't afford in my busy, responsibility filled life. Those beliefs I held about joy kept me in a holding pattern, which made it hard for me to cultivate joy for myself. Unknowingly, I reduced my ability to experience more joy because of fears I'd somehow risk becoming less valuable and less productive.

Notice how I was questioning my own value with this thought process about myself and joy? There was a sense of self-sacrifice going on for me. It was as if I had to endure more hardship to be worthy of experiencing more joy. I didn't realize I was questioning my own value through the lifestyle I'd been living, but I had been. This was an indicator that I was putting conditions on my sense of self-worth, thwarting opportunities to cultivate and experience joy more deeply and more often. As you explore your own joy journey, be vigilant of what hidden beliefs and old thought patterns may be hindering your open-ness to experience more joy.

POINT TO PONDER #38

Joy and Fear

Joy is fun. It feels inspiring and purposeful. It's freeing and light-hearted. It feels like flow. It does not have to be earned. Depending on your own personal history, these kinds of experiences may or may not feel feasible or familiar. You may or may not feel worthy to embrace more of these kinds of experiences. In this exercise, notice what your personal experience and reactions are here. Allow yourself to explore whatever concerns may come up around joy.

Do I have any fears or concerns about experiencing joy? How so? If I were to experience more fun, joy and care-free types of moments, are there any things I worry may happen or might have an undesired impact?

Recite and affirm out loud at least three times today (starting now). Plug a reminder into your phone so you don't forget: "I love welcoming joy into my life. The more joy I have, the more joy I can share!"

It turns out, the more joyful we are, the less stressed we feel, and the more productive we can be! I didn't need to prove anything to be worthy of more joy. Cultivating more joy is something we all can do and are all worthy of. As I started welcoming in more joy, I realized I didn't need to sacrifice my productivity. What I needed to sacrifice was unnecessary stress and control.

Go figure!

Once I shifted my perspective on this, the challenge became figuring out what helped me to cultivate joy! I had spent so much time focused on productivity that I wasn't entirely sure about everything that brought me joy.

Lots of people are unsure about what brings them joy because they spend so much time on the stressful stuff and forget about the fun parts of life. If you're unsure about what may bring you joy, it's understandable. You're not alone in that. We are going to take some time with this today.

POINT TO PONDER #39
What Elicits Joy?

To figure out some things that help bring you joy, I invite you to sit down and really reflect upon what lights you up when you think of or engage with it. Have fun with this activity. It takes time and thoughtful reflection. Allow this to be a joyful exploration! A good way for some people to get started with this process is to look back to when you were a child. Even difficult childhoods can have parts that stand out as feeling joyful in some way. If you're having trouble sorting out the difference between what makes you feel happy and what helps you cultivate joy, don't worry about that right now.

What things did I enjoy engaging in as a child or teen? What was it that really lit me up about those experiences?

What did I get excited about or look forward to? What about it made me feel that way? What did I want to do and be? Why? What felt so inspirational about it all?

_____

_____

_____

_____

_____

_____

_____

_____

_____

_____

_____

_____

_____

_____

_____

Visuals, like photos, often help people with emotionally connecting to prior life experiences. Using the blank space provided in this next section, place photos, drawings or other visuals that help to elicit joy or happiness for you. As you look back through old photos, memories, notebooks, yearbooks, etc., let the emotions you feel guide you as to what you'd like to include. Write down notes about what you notice as you do so.

PICTURES AND MEMORABILIA

PICTURES AND MEMORABILIA

As I reflect on pictures and memories from my life, I notice:

Looking back at what I've written, common themes I see popping up about what I really enjoy now or enjoyed back then are:

_____

_____

_____

_____

_____

_____

_____

_____

_____

The ways I see these themes and reflections connecting with what matters most to me and my life now are:

_____

_____

_____

_____

_____

_____

_____

_____

_____

As you look back at old experiences, you may inadvertently come across some painful times too. Take note of what you learned from those challenges, how you've grown since then, and how your view of the world was shaped by them. It's important to take time and leave space for those experiences if they come up.

Use the prompt below to acknowledge these experiences, and to take your time reflecting on how you've developed since then.

How have any challenging or painful experiences that have come up for me, helped to shape me into the person I am today? In what ways am I proud of the way I've grown or chosen to learn from these times?

_____

_____

_____

_____

_____

_____

_____

_____

_____

_____

_____

_____

_____

Did you take your time with this exercise? If you rushed through it, go back and do it again. Do it as many times as you need before you move forward.

Recite and affirm out loud at least three times today (starting now). Plug a reminder into your phone so you don't forget: "I love welcoming joy into my life. The more joy I have, the more joy I can share!"

CULTIVATING JOY IS NATURAL.

Joy is a natural experience for humans to cultivate because joy is derived from a state of internal wellness. Wellness is a natural state that our brains and bodies strive to be in. So many people forget how to cultivate joy, not because they can't, but because they've just grown so accustomed to *not* living in a state of wellness. Instead, most modern-day people live in a state of constant hustle and bustle, stress, dis-ease or urgency. This leaves a void, which we talked about earlier on in the section on meaningfully connecting. To feel better, we try to fill the void with things or by taking tons of action. This contributes to habits like "shiny object syndrome" or "retail therapy". It extends beyond those habits into an *if I have* or *if I do this, then I'll be happy*...kind of thought process which leads us down an unfulfilling rabbit hole and away from cultivating the joy we want to experience. The ability to cultivate more joy is always there, it just takes a bit of unlearning what society taught us about what's supposed to bring meaning to our lives. It's less about status, stuff or accomplishments and more about fun, purpose and enjoyment.

As you have experienced throughout this process, consistent practice helps to rewire the brain. The benefits of consistency don't only apply to behavioral habits, but to mental habits as well. This means mentally practicing how to cultivate joy is something each of us can do! Remember it's not bland, robotic repetition that does the trick here. Successful change happens when you consistently practice marrying the elevated emotion while repeating the new habit.

We can use this information to our benefit and envision what it feels like to connect with joyful experiences in our minds. The more you do that, the more you feel it, and the more you enhance your practice for welcoming more joy into your life. To help you get the hang of it, I'll walk you through a practice you can engage with on your own. Once you get the hang of it, you can use this practice on your own, as often as you'd like.

JOY PRACTICE

Sit back, close your eyes, and visualize a joyful experience.

What do you see? Notice it. Describe it.

What do you feel in your body or against your skin? Notice it. Describe it.

Who do you notice?

How do you feel? Notice it. Describe it.

What are you doing?

Who are you with?

Where are you?

Notice any tastes or scents.

Notice if you hear anything.

Take your time and enjoy it in your mind for a few moments; the longer, the better.

Enjoy the joy.

Smile.

Recite and affirm out loud at least three times today (starting now). Plug a reminder into your phone so you don't forget: "I love welcoming joy into my life. The more joy I have, the more joy I can share!"

Have you gotten clearer on and more connected with what brings you joy?

Based upon your experiences with your Points to Ponder this week, craft a reference list of what helps you cultivate joy. You can tap into this list at any time to incorporate opportunities for more joyful moments in your life on a more regular basis.

POINT TO PONDER #40
My Reference List of Joys

Recite and affirm out loud at least three times today (starting now). Plug a reminder into your phone so you don't forget: "I love welcoming joy into my life. The more joy I have, the more joy I can share!"

CHAPTER RECAP

Self-love is a foundation for welcoming joy. Joy brings fervor and meaning to life and relationships. However, joy can't be artificially fabricated or forced; to experience more joy, you'll have to really explore how you feel about what and when. This deeper level of self-exploration will help you to unveil opportunities for experiencing more joy in your day to day life, without any need for additional extravagance or copious expenditure of time, resources or energy.

You can connect with joyful moments intentionally and create the capacity to welcome in more and more and more! There is no cap; joy can be experienced in abundance! The more joy you experience, the more you can share in that experience with others!

CHAPTER INSIGHTS

That age-old saying, "The joy is in the journey," rings so true to me—although it didn't always. I used to roll my eyes at it and perceive it as a mere cliché with minimal relevance to me and my life. However, it has a completely different meaning now than it did for me even just a handful of years ago.

How about you?

Consider this thought as you take time to contemplate and reflect upon the prompts below. Write down honest, open, and reflective responses in the space provided.

Am I truly welcoming joy into my life? Do I have a better idea of how to cultivate more experiences of joy now, than I did before?

Am I committed to practicing joyful moments in my mind, even when life itself isn't filled with joyful-type circumstances? Why or why not? What might make this hard, and what could I do about it?

_____

_____

_____

_____

_____

_____

_____

_____

_____

_____

_____

_____

_____

_____

BONUS CHALLENGE.

Remind yourself you deserve to feel more joy and put it into practice. Schedule at least two things from your reference list of joys to engage in this upcoming week.

Recite and affirm out loud at least three times today (starting now). Plug a reminder into your phone so you don't forget: "I love welcoming joy into my life. The more joy I have, the more joy I can share!"

Chapter Nine:

Core Concept Eight: The Reality Check

You're in a different place now than you were before you started your RESET journey. Things have changed. You've shifted in meaningful ways—perhaps some subtle and some overt.

At this point in your RESET process, it's time to take note of how far you've come. Taking time to acknowledge where you were and where you are now helps to reinforce the efforts you've put in. It helps you want to keep going so you can continue to progress.

It's a reality check for yourself.

Your reality check will help you see where you're presently at and what you need to do next to continue welcoming the life experiences you want. It's not intended to be used to beat yourself up for anything that has not gone exactly how you'd hoped. To do so would be counterproductive. This reality check provides an opportunity to celebrate how you've grown, to experience more appreciation for the process you've committed to, and to help you continue your expansion moving forward. It's a beautiful and powerful thing.

My reality check brought to my attention where I was growing and reminded me of my strengths. It also gave me helpful hints of what challenging areas to stay cognizant of so they'd be less likely to sneak back into my life and relationships. I noticed I'd made great strides with trusting myself, taking more time for my own needs, and even made progress in setting boundaries. This reflection led me to feel so grateful for how much closer to myself I had become. However, the area of trusting *others* was still hard for me. I worried about getting taken advantage of and hurt like I had experienced in the past. I realized trust was something I needed to continue to pay attention to and refocus on more deliberately. I wanted to continue to grow there so I could learn to trust others more, which would further enhance my relationships.

When I work with clients, I strategically take time to go back and review their initial goals and challenges from when they first came to me. Without fail, the contrast between where they are in their journey and where they were when they began, brings about a potent experience that serves as a positive influence for them.

It could do the same for you.

POINT TO PONDER #41
RESET Review + Reflect

To appreciate how far you've come, it's often helpful to remind yourself of where you were. In the first week of your RESET process, you wrote down what you no longer wanted to experience. To kick off your reality check for this chapter, go back to your notes from the beginning of your RESET, where you wrote out your *don't wants*. Review them.

As you look at what you no longer wanted to experience, notice what comes up for you. Take note of how you have shifted since then, both inwardly (how you feel and perceive) and outwardly (changes you've seen happen outside of yourself, like in relationships or particular situations). Write down your reflections below:

Continue to reflect. Ask yourself:

How have I progressed in areas related to my health, my relationships, my work, my emotion management, my communication, my energy, or my time management?

_____

_____

_____

_____

_____

_____

_____

_____

_____

_____

_____

_____

_____

_____

_____

_____

_____

_____

Whatever you noticed in this reflection is okay. Even if you notice you've made progress in some areas and not so much progress in other areas. It's all part of your ongoing process. Being aware of where you've made progress as well as where and how you'd like to continue making progress is just the reality check you need to tend to the next parts of your journey.

Memory is fickle. You can't rely on memory alone to account for the progress and shifts you've made. Giving yourself the credit due for the efforts you've put in will help you feel more motivated, inspired, and confident in continuing to grow and move along in your journey. You'll be asked to actively explore your growth throughout this reality check chapter. Let's see what you continue to notice.

Recite and affirm out loud at least three times today (starting now). Plug a reminder into your phone so you don't forget: "I'm getting better and better at allowing what I desire. I choose to trust the process."

By the time I'd allowed myself to:

Disconnect from what I didn't want (and what didn't need to matter so much to me anymore),

Connect with what I did want and how I wanted to be,

Reconnect with a supportive power much greater than myself, and

Practiced cultivating joy more intentionally,

I felt freer, clearer and more joyful.

You, too, have allowed yourself to disconnect from what you don't want and what doesn't need to be most important so you can connect with what you do want, how you do want to be, and what does matter most to you. You've connected or reconnected with a power much greater than yourself, yet supportive from within, and you've chosen to cultivate more joy in your life.

It's not possible for this process to *not* have an impact on you or your life.

So, how do you feel?

Let's explore this a bit more in the next exercise.

POINT TO PONDER #42
Joyful Clarity!

You've moved along this journey to hit your RESET button by following powerful core concepts and targeting essential areas of your life that call for your attention. Are you beginning to feel freer? Have you gained any clarity? Have you opened yourself up to experience a bit more joyfulness? Take time today to reflect on this.

How am I feeling at this point in my RESET journey?

How often am I feeling this way?

In general, what am I most frequently feeling? Does it feel good? Insightful? Powerful? Something else?

What feels or seems different for me now, no matter how small or slight it may appear on the surface?

At this point, do I believe that how I feel matters? Why or why not?

_____

_____

_____

_____

What other thoughts, reactions, experiences, or feelings have I noticed being stirred up within me recently?

_____

_____

_____

_____

Here are some prompts to help you go deeper with this check-in:

I have been feeling more and more

_____

_____

_____

I have noticed a feeling of _____

_____

and I think it's _____

_____.

Recite and affirm out loud at least three times today (starting now). Plug a reminder into your phone so you don't forget: "I'm getting better and better at allowing what I desire. I choose to trust the process."

Part of your reality check is getting super clear about the benefits you've gained from making a commitment to yourself. As I reflected on the many benefits I'd experienced in various aspects of my life, I grew more and more appreciative. I felt more hopeful, thankful, and positive.

When you take time to reality check what's going well, you reinforce your desired benefits of your RESET. This will increase the likelihood that you'll choose to take what you've learned here and continue to apply it in your life as you move forward.

POINT TO PONDER #43
Self-Growth Check-in

How have I seen or experienced growth and benefits in each of these areas of my life these past two months? How have I been dealing with stressors in each of these areas?

My Professional/Work Life (i.e. organization, stress or time management, relationships and performance).

My Family Life (i.e relationships, parenting, communication, stress and conflict management):

_____

_____

_____

_____

_____

_____

_____

_____

_____

_____

_____

_____

_____

_____

_____

_____

_____

_____

_____

_____

My Personal Life (i.e. friendships, fun, rest and relaxation, hobbies, stress management, self-care):

_____

_____

_____

_____

_____

_____

_____

_____

_____

_____

_____

_____

_____

_____

_____

_____

_____

_____

Recite and affirm out loud at least three times today (starting now). Plug a reminder into your phone so you don't forget: "I'm getting better and better at allowing what I desire. I choose to trust the process."

WEEDING AND SEEDING.

How's your reality check going so far?

As I went through it, I noticed more and more about who and what was in my life that I didn't align with. The closer I felt to me, the more evident it was when other relationships or things seemed off in my life. There were certain relationships, and certain lifestyle choices I could feel were not expanding with me as I grew. To figure out how to navigate it, I had to reality check myself. It seemed, with my newfound sense of self and purpose, I needed to get more deliberate about where and with whom I was spending my time, energy, and efforts. This was an especially challenging part for me.

As you continue along your own self-development path, you'll grow in your own sense of discernment about what feels aligned and what feels off for you too. This will be especially true with regard to relationships and your own mental and behavioral patterns.

Throughout my RESET journey, some of the people and things that weren't aligned with the healthier direction I was headed in just naturally weeded themselves out. But that wasn't the case for all of them. There were other things and relationships that required me to address them more specifically. I had to figure out which ones to get more deliberate about addressing (so they could grow too) and which ones I simply needed to move on from. I call this process "weeding and seeding".

Weeding means no longer allowing certain things in your life, like particularly unhealthy relationships or behaviors. These may be toxic relationships that you can feel even more strongly now, so you know you need to remove yourself from them. Alternatively, there may be a pattern of behaviors that you yourself need to weed out and let go of.

Seeding means noticing what feels off and deliberately addressing it to help bring it up to speed with who you are now. You consciously choose to introduce more of what you want to grow in place of that "off-ness." This may look like, for example, you've become more aware of on-going, constant misunderstanding in a certain relationship and it feels off or out of sync with who and how you are now. Rather than do nothing or grow miserable about it, you may get more intentional about how to address it. Perhaps you choose to have a much-needed open and honest conversation while simultaneously demonstrating more compassion as you engage in that relationship.

At this point in my journey, feeling "off" was enough for me to know I needed to pay attention and discern if there was some weeding or seeding that needed to happen. If I had felt the "off-ness" but didn't do anything about it, then I would have felt more disconnected from myself, my core values and my missing link. If I'd started feeling disconnected, then I wasn't being deliberate about my RESET. If I was feeling disconnected, not being deliberate about my RESET and chose not to do anything about it, then I wouldn't be staying true to who I am and the person I desire to be. That was no longer an option for me. That form of self-neglect was a betrayal I'd experienced before and had committed to no longer do to myself.

No matter what kind of RESET you desire for yourself, it's important you don't ignore any ongoing *off-ness* that you feel happening in your life. Some things, people, and situations will naturally fade themselves out. Other times, you will have to get intentional and decide whether it's time for you to weed or seed certain relationships, behaviors, etc. By practicing doing so, you're practicing staying true to who you desire to be for your life and your RESET.

POINT TO PONDER #44
Weed and Seed

The weed and seed process often connects with specific relationships in our lives. As a social species, our relationships are impacted as we develop ourselves. Whether your RESET was directly related to specific relationships or not, take a moment to reflect on how you're experiencing relationships as you've developed along your RESET process.

Is the relationship I have with myself supporting my RESET process? Yes or no. How so?

Is the way I relate to and socialize with others supporting my RESET process? How so? Why or why not?

_____

_____

_____

_____

_____

_____

_____

_____

_____

_____

_____

_____

_____

_____

_____

_____

_____

_____

_____

Is there is an "off-ness" being felt in any relationship (including the one with myself)? Have I done anything about it so far? Do I want to? Why or why not?

Am I feeling good about where my relationships are currently? How am I feeling about where they are headed?

Have some relationships naturally shifted as a result of my growth? Which ones? In what ways?

Do I need to weed out certain relationships that I can feel are off?

Do I want to plant some seeds within certain relationships?

_____

_____

_____

_____

_____

_____

_____

_____

_____

_____

_____

_____

_____

_____

_____

_____

_____

_____

Recite and affirm out loud at least three times today (starting now). Plug a reminder into your phone so you don't forget: "I'm getting better and better at allowing what I desire. I choose to trust the process."

As I continued to grow closer to myself, I continued to notice that my friendships were changing. My interactions with people were changing. There was naturally less interaction with some people. I initially felt saddened by this in some instances because I value connections with people. However, after I reality checked myself, I realized the natural weeding-out process was occurring because I'd changed. I was in a different place in my life. I was in a different headspace. I was on a different path. Some relationships simply were not able to be held in this new space; they didn't match-up with the healthier direction I was moving in.

It's possible you may feel guilt, grief or sadness about the weeding out process. Many people do. There were certainly moments when I felt guilty for stepping away from certain people and places. Sometimes I needed to take time to grieve and let myself feel sad. But the truth is your self-growth, health and happiness is not a bad or wrong thing to prioritize. I learned that this is easier said than done; yet it needed to be experienced by me. Today I can say with confidence that it would have done me no good to stay stuck where I was just because others wanted me to. Not everyone is ready to heal or evolve themselves at the same time or in the same way. We each have our own journey to experience. In fact, the example I offered through the life course I chose to chart, was far more beneficial to those who were stuck than I ever could have been had I never RESET.

The more I valued myself and my boundaries, the more relationships that didn't value them began to either change or naturally shift out of my life. I could feel healthier relationships begin to form and take hold. I'd also become more adept at spotting unhealthy patterns; I noticed them viscerally. This made it hard not to notice the relationships with unhealthy patterns that hadn't naturally shifted out of my life experience. I had to decide if I would weed them out on purpose or if I needed to get even more intentional about how to practice healthier interactions within those relationships.

While the weed and seed process is generally necessary and can often unfold naturally, the parts that are left for us to address ourselves do take time and intention. Family relationships, for example, are often an area where you may have to get even more deliberate. When it comes to family, it can be tough to discern if relationships with unhealthy patterns need to be weeded out or seeded in. In some very challenging cases, some people do decide to weed toxic family relationships out completely or to significantly reduce exposure to them for a period of time. That may be what you choose to do if it fits for you. Others choose to get even more intentional about incorporating within certain relationships what they've learned about themselves through the RESET, and that helps shift the relationship dynamics over time. No one else can tell you what is right for you here. You have to decide where to weed and when to seed. Seeding new or different interactions happens when you intentionally target and address the "off-ness" you feel within the relationship (like boundary-violations, unclear communication, etc.).

Healthy relationships require healthy boundaries, and if you're feeling any "off-ness" in a relationship, a boundary may need to be addressed. You've likely explored boundaries throughout your RESET process already (I know I did!), so you're more aware of them now.

Today is a good day to reality check where your boundaries are and aren't within your relationships (including your relationship with yourself).

POINT TO PONDER #45
Reality Checking Boundaries

What are some boundaries that are working for me? In what ways are they working?

Are any of those boundaries newly improved or newly laid out? Are some harder than others?

_____

_____

_____

_____

_____

_____

_____

_____

_____

_____

_____

_____

_____

_____

_____

_____

_____

_____

_____

Have I decided to weed out or plant seeds into any relationships? If so, what boundaries will I need to explore? Why?

What are two or three ways I may manage any barriers to implementing some of these boundaries?

Recite and affirm out loud at least three times today (starting now). Plug a reminder into your phone so you don't forget: "I'm getting better and better at allowing what I desire. I choose to trust the process."

In the last section, we focused mostly on the relational piece of your reality check. Relationships are how we connect with the world around us; they help us co-create so many different things and experiences in various areas of our life. If we are unwilling to clarify whether they are aligned with how we want to show up within this world, we are significantly limiting ourselves on so many levels. If you did not take the time to explore these relational pieces yet, do that before proceeding.

The weeding and seeding process is not a one-and-done thing. The decision to weed out or plant more seeds into any relationship will be ongoing. Although we have already dug into your beliefs and behavior patterns, you can reinforce your growth in those areas by applying the weed and seed process to your mental habits and behavioral patterns as well. A thought that I needed to further weed out was me needing to do everything on my own. The more I repeated that old thought to myself, the more I believed it. If I were to rewire that belief system even more than I had up until that point in my journey, then I needed to do some additional weeding of the thought.

In this next section, you're going to get curious about whether your mental habits and lifestyle (behavioral) choices may be hindering progress for your growth and your RESET. It's important to notice if certain habits may be blocking you from letting in some more of your desired experiences. If you don't identify them, you won't adequately address them.

Say you were initially seeking a RESET because you wanted to have a better relationship with your partner or your kids. You have been focusing on that desire throughout your RESET process. However, you also have a habit of eating junk food and staying up late every night. The desire and the behavior pattern may seem unrelated, but they impact one another.

Allow me to illustrate.

Perhaps you feel stressed after a day in the life of parenting and marriage, so you stay up late for some "me time". However, when you stay up so late, you wind up eating junk food. As a result, you don't get the amount of sleep you wanted, and you're frustrated with yourself about the weight you keep gaining. All too often, you wake up irritated and tired. When you wake up irritated and tired, it becomes harder to have patience with your kids and partner. Although you've made some progress with managing your irritation, you may feel like you've hit a wall with breaking this vicious cycle. Unintentionally, the night time behavior habits are impacting the relational interactions with your partner and kids.

In this next exercise, you'll be getting curious and asking yourself if these nighttime behavioral habits are really in alignment with the experiences you desire to have more of in your life.

While it may seem daunting to address certain behavior patterns that have been on-going for you, we always have the opportunity to learn and grow. This is without exception. In brain science this capability is called neuroplasticity. In this context, neuroplasticity basically means that across your lifespan you can rewire your brain to support you differently. No matter your age or history, you still get to learn and grow if you so desire. Since no one is perfect or omnipotent, we will all have habits (mental and behavioral) in need of some assessing and addressing at some point throughout our lives. Rest assured that having habits in need of shifting does not mean anything is bad, wrong, or broken about you. Although we all have the power to benefit from neuroplasticity, it's up to you as an individual whether or not you'll consciously put in the effort to take advantage of your brain's neuroplastic power.

Mental and behavioral habits are not bad to have. It's just that some are working for you right now and some are not. Your habits can be healthy and serve you very well. Just as important as it is to be aware of an unhealthy habit so you can shift it, it's equally helpful to be aware of a habit or lifestyle choice that feels good and does good for you. Learn which habits effectively help you to experience more of what you want to experience in life. Creating new, healthy habits that work for you, is a form of seeding. Changing old habits that are not working for you, is a form of weeding.

POINT TO PONDER #46
Reality Check My RESET

Deepen your reality check by going back to chapter three. Review the experiences you **do** want more of. As you do so, reflect on your current mental and behavioral habits. Get curious as to whether your current lifestyle reflects the experiences you said you wanted to create more of. Take time to remind yourself of what you wanted to *feel* more of.

Note what sticks out to you:

_____

_____

_____

_____

_____

_____

_____

_____

_____

_____

_____

_____

_____

_____

_____

_____

_____

_____

Then, ask yourself:

- Am I allowing these desired experiences to gradually be felt by me, more and more?
- How have I been creating opportunities for me to experience these more?
- What kinds of thoughts have I been repeating to myself that seem in line with these desires?

After you have completed the above steps, answer the below questions honestly and openly:

What behaviors/actions/decisions have I been making that are allowing me to experience more of this? Are there certain habits that've been helping me experience more of what I want? Do I want to continue them? Why or why not?

Are there certain lifestyle habits I choose to change, stop, or reduce in my life? Why or why not? What difference could it make for me? My health? My happiness?

_____

_____

_____

_____

_____

_____

_____

_____

_____

_____

_____

_____

_____

_____

_____

_____

_____

_____

Recite and affirm out loud at least three times today (starting now). Plug a reminder into your phone so you don't forget: "I'm getting better and better at allowing what I desire. I choose to trust the process."

You're approaching the last session of your RESET! Congratulations! Yes, I'm congratulating you again, and I encourage you to do the same for yourself. Taking time to celebrate your efforts and growth will help your brain keep doing more explorative self-work. Initially, it felt weird for me to celebrate myself. I was used to pushing myself hard and overextending myself for everyone else, so it felt incredibly uncomfortable to congratulate myself for slowing down and prioritizing myself. I can tell you when I stopped making myself wrong for taking care of me and I let myself receive the congratulations, it felt better. Do yourself a favor and genuinely care about all the progress as well as the challenges you've navigated. You'll greatly benefit from it.

Okay, now onto the next part of your reality check.

As you've reality checked yourself, your relationships, and your habits this week, you may or may not have also become more aware of who and what has drained you. Some people call these kinds of draining interactions an "energy suck." We all have had some experience with it. You engaged with someone or something, and when you walked away you couldn't help but feel depleted.

These kinds of engagements are important to note so you can explore what may not be aligned within you and within the context of the relationship, action, or thing. You've already begun to do some of the work on this within this chapter. You want to know who and what is draining your energy so you can address it. If you notice some energy sucking going on, go back to the weed and seed exercise and apply it here.

And of course, as is the case throughout your RESET, the people, places and things leaving you feel the opposite of an "energy suck" matter here too. You want to know who and what is enhancing your life and your energy because you want to spend more time appreciating them. Therefore, it's equally important to increase awareness of the energy-giving relationships, things, and actions—the people and things that are cup fillers.

POINT TO PONDER #47

Energy Depleting or Energy Giving?

Get curious about what is sucking your energy and what is filling up your cup. If there is too much draining going on, you will not show up as your best self. If your cup is often filled, you will have more to give and more to enjoy.

Are there any energy sucking, or depleting kinds of interactions I'm often having with certain people, places or things? If yes, how so? How often? How might I be contributing to these exchanges?

How might I apply the concept of "weed or seed" for the engagements that are too often draining me?

What people, places or actions do I engage with and leave feeling filled up? *(I.e cousin, mountains and gardening).*

_____

_____

_____

_____

_____

_____

_____

_____

_____

Am I enjoying these relationships, places and/or things to do, and appreciating what they offer me? How so? What am I mostly appreciative of about them?

_____

_____

_____

_____

_____

_____

_____

_____

_____

_____

Am I an equal contributor to these people, places and/or things? Is there a symbiotic type of relationship happening? Can there be? Am I okay with this? Why or why not?

_____

_____

_____

_____

_____

_____

_____

_____

Generally speaking, do I consider myself to be a cup filler in life? Am I also a receiver? Do I allow myself to be filled up while also allowing myself to share out my energy in a way that benefits other people, places or things? If no, why not? If yes, how so?

_____

_____

_____

_____

_____

_____

_____

_____

_____

_____

_____

_____

_____

_____

_____

_____

_____

_____

Recite and affirm out loud at least three times today (starting now). Plug a reminder into your phone so you don't forget: "I'm getting better and better at allowing what I desire. I choose to trust the process."

CHAPTER RECAP

CONGRATULATIONS!

You reality-tested your desires, your progress, your relationships, and your habits this week. Reality testing is so important because it allows you to reinforce what is good and helpful and release and address what is not good or helpful for you and your RESET.

If you skipped through this chapter or did not take it seriously enough, I strongly encourage you to go back and engage with every single lesson and prompt thoughtfully. Every time you participate in an exercise, no matter how long or short, you're likely to notice something different. Take your time and meaningfully engage. Don't rush. It's easy to sweep right through this last chapter and not fully reality test yourself. But, if you choose to do that, you will only be selling yourself short.

Take your time. How you choose to spend your time impacts how you experience your life.

CHAPTER INSIGHTS

Take time to contemplate and reflect upon these questions. Write down honest, open, and reflective responses in the space provided.

Did I meaningfully and honestly reflect upon the lessons, questions, and prompts in this chapter?

Did I reality-test myself and get clearer on the progress I've made as well as the areas that need to be more intentionally addressed? How so? Can I provide evidence to support this response? If yes, what did I gain from it? If no, why? What got in the way?

Recite and affirm out loud at least three times today (starting now). Plug a reminder into your phone so you don't forget: "I'm getting better and better at allowing what I desire. I choose to trust the process."

You did it!

You RESET!

You hit your RESET button!

How will you celebrate yourself and your RESET?

CELEBRATE!

You've created a new baseline for yourself and your life! You've hit your RESET button and have RESET yourself at a place of enhanced development. Self growth is an ongoing process; it's never done. The benefits of this RESET process will continue forevermore. Your opportunities to RESET and grow are endless! Therefore, you'll likely want to hit your RESET button again in the future. Or perhaps you'd like to go through it again simply to go deeper in a different area of your life. That's a good thing. Much like rereading a book or re-watching a movie, new things will become evident to you when you choose to hit your RESET button again. You'll benefit differently each time. I know I do!

Closing

I feel such deep appreciation for you. I don't say that lightly. This RESET process is undeniably powerful and requires a level of self-exploration and reflection that most would be wary to venture. I'm so grateful that you've chosen to share this part of your life journey with me.

If you desire to go deeper with self-development that enhances all aspects of living, I invite you to join us in the new RESET community which is currently being held on Facebook. The URL is https://www.facebook.com/groups/lifesresetbutton. For additional support on how to shift your time, effort, and energy in a way you're aligned with, I welcome you to check out www.BoldAndBalancedCoaching.Com. There you'll find a variety of free resources and premium services like coaching courses, presentations, books, consulting options and limited opportunities to work privately with me. Each of these are intermittently updated to best serve leaders and impact-makers like you, so I can't guarantee what will be available or when.

If you know you need the boost that only premium accountability and support can provide, I invite you to explore what premium mentorship options may be available at this time. If you choose to pursue this route, know that you always have choices. It's important you find a mentor, therapist or professional that you feel connected with as you commit to your ongoing development. If you want to have me in your back pocket as an honest teacher, experienced guide and compassionate confidant while you further enhance your personal and professional growth journey, exclusive opportunities to work one-on-one with me are sometimes available. You can apply at www.BoldAndBalancedCoaching.Com.

Be proud. You officially hit your RESET button!

Your life is meant to be enjoyed.

A successful life is a life that's been well-lived, filled with meaningful connection, meaningful contribution, faith, love and variety. It's not about just getting things done or just getting through. So, go out and live!

— Dr. Toni

Connecting Further

For speaking engagements, coaching courses or private mentorship, please visit BoldandBalancedCoaching.com

*Your quality of life is dictated much less by what you're doing,
and much more by why you're doing it.
Realizing why you're living life the way you are will change you,
everyone around you, and it'll change the world for generations to come.
That's the power of your ripple effect.
Use it wisely.*

— Dr. Toni